THE DEATH OF BEST PRACTICES

The Death

of

Best Practices

REIMAGINING HR THROUGH

CULTIVATING A GROWTH MINDSET

Susan P. Chen, PhD

HOUNDSTOOTH
PRESS

THE DEATH OF BEST PRACTICES
Reimagining HR through Cultivating a Growth Mindset

FIRST EDITION

ISBN   978-1-5445-3795-5 *Hardcover*
       978-1-5445-3793-1 *Paperback*
       978-1-5445-3794-8 *Ebook*

Contents

Introduction

In 2016, after more than a decade spent living in mature market bubbles like the United Kingdom, Norway, and Singapore, I relocated to Indonesia as the chief human resources officer (CHRO) for a healthcare startup. The job required a complete business model and human resources (HR) transformation under the close watch of investors.

Soon, I was back in Singapore for an HR conference. I was excited by the thought of a functional mass rapid transit and non-congested roads, as well as the potential to learn and reconnect with HR colleagues from comparatively more mature markets. I really wanted to see how I could adapt what I learnt to some of the challenges I faced in Indonesia.

At the conference, there was much excitement and buzz, especially on how technology would continue to transform how to *do* HR. I chuckled at how we often say, "doing HR," indicating that HR is inherently understood as an activity rather than a practice or a highly skilled profession that works with complex people-related issues.

"You should create a special app to recruit top talent," an in-house recruitment lead from a leading Asian bank suggested to me. "Oh, you *have to* create a new technology experience for recruiting; that is key," he added excitedly.

I hummed, nodded, and gave him a tiny smile, as though I agreed with him. Internally, though, I sighed. This was not the first conversation I found myself trapped in while attending one of the largest conferences for HR leaders in Asia. Hundreds of us had gathered to share and learn the best practices for virtual recruitment and engagement. I was not surprised or particularly captivated by this man's suggestion—it rang too familiar. I had heard variations of his idea and others like it from attendee after attendee, all eager to share what had worked for them at their companies.

I wandered that conference in Singapore, sat in on panel discussions, traded ideas with attendees, and listened to more conversations about the best practices for recruiting and retaining talent. None of the suggestions I heard were revolutionary, groundbreaking, or outside the box. Sure, people had achieved strong results with these practices, but my HR colleagues were missing one monumental detail: we were focused on the *what*. The activities, the ready-made solutions, the tested and proven programs.

No one was asking the bigger question: *how?* How should we approach the challenges in our operational contexts without a fixed solution in mind?

My counterparts and I not only worked for companies in Asia; many of us worked in emerging markets where the cultures, governments, markets, and talent landscapes were different. What worked in a mature American or European market was not going to work in countries like Indonesia, Malaysia, China, or Singapore. But few, if any, of my HR counterparts at the conference had overtly expressed or addressed the diversity of these markets and the potential need to approach them differently.

Like the recruiter who suggested I use a special app to recruit talent, most attendees assumed that the way to recruit talent was through technology. That is true—as long as the talent base is largely connected to the internet. I had used creative virtual recruitment strategies while working for companies in the United Kingdom and Norway. In those countries, everyone has a personal computer, tablet, or smartphone. Most people have all three.

Indonesia, on the other hand, is a country that boasts a population of approximately 240 million people, yet only roughly 80 million are connected to the internet. That amounts to only about *33 per cent of the population.* Of that 33 per cent, I have no idea how many are active job seekers. It is also a country in which 300 different dialects are spoken! Building a recruitment strategy via a creative app and technology was not the way to reach my talent base in Indonesia, even though that would have been considered the best practice to use.

This conference marked a turning point, as it kick-started the ideation for this book. It was the moment I realised that the HR best practices that many (myself included) had studied, pursued, and used in our careers were not failsafe for those of us working in emerging Asia. In fact, they were what was holding us back from achieving sustainable results for our companies. It was not just the best practices themselves that bothered me but the mindset of the one-size-fits-all approach—the idea that what worked for another organisation would, by definition, work for mine.

I started this manuscript in 2016 with the emerging market in mind, and I wanted to call out the intricacies and ineffectiveness of our current approach by referring to the best practices of mature markets as the HR best practice playbook for emerging markets. The manuscript was completed at the end of 2018. However, I came to a further realisation that suggesting an emerging market alternative to best practices only builds on the assumption of best practices as ready-made solutions for certain similar contexts.

Then—everything changed.

The year 2021 was unprecedented for many of us. As I write this, the coronavirus pandemic is sweeping the world, and the future of work appears more uncertain than ever. Many look to the HR function for support and guidance. At the same time, HR as a profession and function continues to transform and, for the most part, struggles to deliver on the promise of a brighter, more flexible, and deeply engaged future workforce.

The global pandemic is not only a public health emergency but a political, economic, and social emergency in which many of our deep-rooted beliefs are being questioned and solutions are being redefined. HR's role is, indeed, evolving. Consultant and author David Ulrich recognised this twenty years ago, and more people are seeing the possibilities—even governments.

"We must make an effort to raise the level of HR practice in Singapore. It is not easy for individuals to adjust to constant and rapid change on their own," said Singapore Prime Minister Lee Hsien Loong right before the pandemic hit. "A strong and capable HR community can be the catalyst and change agent to initiate and implement people-development efforts in organisations and help build stronger capabilities amongst our business leaders and managers."

Following this announcement, Singapore's government introduced an HR competency framework—one of the first of its kind.

This book seeks to take a more reflective and introspective approach to the practice of HR. It is written by an HR practitioner for HR practitioners, and it comes from a deep-rooted optimism that HR is at the forefront of the next wave of changes, accelerated by the pandemic and a shift in our fundamental work structure. Now, it is even more important that HR leaders not only see the possibilities, but that they practise a different way of thinking and working together to run and own business performance.

If HR leaders must evolve as our roles evolve, how can we break free from a best practice mindset to start thinking with a growth mindset and with a growth practice in mind?

Some have pointed out that the use of the word "death" seems unnecessary and dramatic. The pandemic's lasting impact on the workforce is still hugely unknown. The only thing we do know is that no one will ever go back to the way we were.

The past way of working, as we know it, is dead.

Without trying to evoke panic, I want this book's title to represent both the urgency of change for HR as a profession and the need for us to move away from the comfort zone of best practices. Growth-minded HR does not rely on best practices but uses a combination of different skillsets and tools anchored by a growth mindset to achieve sustainable outcomes for oneself, one's teams, and one's organisation.

This book is a journey of the growth mindset in exploration and practice, and it took more than four years to evolve from ideation to completion. The learnings captured in this book will take you through some of my personal and professional journeys. I started writing, and before I knew it, two more years had passed, I had taken on two more jobs and moves, one psychology degree, and one baby. I then decided to take some time to reflect and begin the daunting task of book revision.

This time, I asked myself, "What mindset do I want to have as an HR professional when I am solving complex and contextual people problems?" What you are reading took shape from there.

The thesis of the book speaks to the next generation of impactful HR practices that will be centred around our ability to look beyond best practices by offering organisational and people solutions that are problem-focused and by channelling a growth mindset in our daily practices. We will also explore what this means more on the individual level. I believe that we can transform the HR function through a collective mindset shift and a change in our individual practices. This book will dive into the growth mindset as a combination of curiosity and grit, offering a clear link between these attributes while attempting to draw out the implications as individuals and as HR leaders.

I like to think of HR practices just like a yoga practice, wherein we continue to develop and hone our skills with incremental but meaningful changes, leading us to transformational enlightenment.

Thus, this book combines my two passions: HR as a profession and learning as a growth mindset that can be developed and practised. This book takes the view that the fundamental role of HR is as a sustainable problem solver. The way to activate and achieve this is through cultivating a growth mindset, engaging curiosity, and practising deep learning.

Best practices are not only a set of proven approaches and tools for HR, but they are also a product of a fixed mindset with many limitations. This book is written with modern HR leaders in mind. In many instances in this book, you can replace "HR" with "people managers" or "leaders," and the messages will still ring true.

THIS BOOK HAS THREE PARTS

The first part leans heavily on curated research and existing thought leadership, but it also offers new perspectives on growth practices. There are various points of view on HR transformation and some case studies to illustrate those points. The second part centres around curiosity and grit as the levers to cultivate a growth mindset. The third part brings it all together and dives deeper into practical strategies for HR leaders to consider how they can transform and develop into a growth mindset HR. Essentially, the three parts of the book can be read independently, and each aims to use strategies as trigger points for reflective inquiry activities and action planning.

Best practices are not golden rules. They are not written-in-stone directives that must be followed. Instead, they are powerful tools to be wielded as necessary to achieve goals. Best practices are merely one approach to address a problem or to achieve a desired result. When HR leaders realise that there are, in fact, many solutions to use, like different tools in a tool chest, a world of possibility opens before them.

For most HR leaders, best practices have become a mindset. The good news is that mindsets can be broken and reshaped. The question, though, is *how?* How do we break free from the best practice mentality?

Breaking from the best practice mindset is not optional—it is imperative.

In short, the heart of this book is about redefining problem-solving through grit and curiosity. A growth mindset is exactly that: problem-solving, redefined.

ON TERMS

This book makes reference to a variety of terms. Without trying to dilute the complexity or evolution these terms carry, I will be referring to HR leaders/practitioners as "HR leaders," to management as "people managers," and to business leaders and companies as "organisations."

I frequently use the term "growth-minded HR" to describe HR leaders with strong growth mindsets.

"Operating environment" refers to the broader context of work that differentiates the experiences of an HR leader. It could refer to organisational size or culture and is used as a way to capture the complexity and differences of the environment in which HR leaders operate. The operating environment often influences the HR leader's approach to problem-solving.

I also make reference to the "market," with the implication that markets represent certain characteristics, such as maturity differences or differences in access to capabilities. I will refer to and make general comparisons between emerging and mature markets as a way to illustrate that the concept of growth-mindset HR is not only applicable in emerging markets. It also holds true for—and is perhaps even more applicable to—mature markets. The market reference may feel generalised, but by no means do I ignore the complexity each market represents and experiences. However, that is not the central thesis of this book.

I also refer to "people/organisation solutions" more generically in reference to the solutions to employee/business-related issues, which could be in the form of HR initiatives at scale or a more individualised application.

The book will offer many reflective inquiry questions throughout instead of offering answers. This is by design, as I want to offer space to trigger thought processes and serve as a starting point for growth practice journeys as HR leaders.

Lastly, you may also find that the book is Asia-centric, providing examples that challenge the status quo in Asia. This is partly due to the fact that I spent the last decade in Asia, but it is also due to the complexity of the markets. These complex markets beautifully illustrate the macro trends described above and are the centre points for continuous HR transformation. Asia is also a hotbed for conventional HR solutions. We still hear many organisations referring to HR as administrative counterparts, and we still field strong demands for best practices.

We are now seeing a trend of referring to "next practices," but our challenge is in how we leapfrog from best practices to growth practices, rather than completely rethinking HR solutions as going from best to next. Best practices are the *what*, and mindsets are the *how*.

This book presents the view that we must approach challenges structurally through a mindset shift to growth practices.

HOW TO APPROACH REFLECTIVE
INQUIRY PRACTICES IN THIS BOOK

Each of the strategies outlined in this book comes with reflective inquiry practices for you to consider to trigger reflections. You do not need to answer all the questions at once or ask them in the order presented.

The questions are positioned in a way that allows you to reflect and experience the impact of self-reflective inquiries. They also serve as blueprints for you to refine and create questions that are intuitive and appropriate for your settings.

PART I

HR Transformation — A Transformation that Never Ends

I am often left speechless when people ask me to explain—really explain—what being in HR means. What is my actual job and impact?

When was the last time you heard a child say, "I want to grow up to be in HR"?

My favourite aunt assumes my job relates to being a secretary to the CEO, helping to manage people-related paperwork. My husband (then boyfriend, oh, what a great first date conversation about our careers!) assumed that my job was more operational and tactical around hiring and firing. Do not even get me started on explaining to my mother why I have countless meetings with CEOs and travel around the region to partner with the business heads on business expansion.

One of my favourite questions happened at a professional networking dinner. A well-mannered and well-dressed man sitting next to me—a corporate business development director, I seem to recall—heard that I am a head of HR with a PhD in the dinner introductions by the host. He shared with me later at dinner with a genuine surprise and shock that there is contemporary education at the bachelor level that could lead to a fulfilling career in HR backed by academic rigour of a PhD.

"Wow," he said. "I did not know HR can be a strategic career!"

These interactions remind me of how HR, as a profession, continues to bring an air of mystery and confusion, anchored on a somewhat misguided perception of our craft. Worst of all, some of these misconceptions and questions are posed by our very own future HR professionals and future key business stakeholders we seek to partner with.

With all this in mind, Chapter 1 of the book will walk through a brief history of HR transformations. This walkthrough serves as a reminder of how the HR profession continues to change and how the complex nature of our role continues to reflect on the fluid nature of the future under the fourth industrialisation. This part of the book will reflect on the changing role of HR within each of the industrial time periods and set the scene for us to reimagine HR. We will also spend some time in this chapter providing connections on the way forward for HR leaders to make an impact by developing a growth mindset—and celebrating the death of best practices. We will walk through how the sentiment of the inadequacy of best practices is shared by Dave Ulrich, a renowned HR researcher and professor, as well as clarify the often-confusing conceptualisation of HR philosophies and the HR operating model.

In Chapter 2, we will dive deeper into moving from "best practices" to "growth practices" and challenge you to reimagine some of the standard people/organisational solutions of present-day HR practices by removing the myths around WOW practices. We will then end Part I of this book with a deeper reflection on how HR can transform as a function.

Are you ready to embark on this learning journey with me?

CHAPTER 1

A Glimpse into the Historical Evolution of HR — Past, Present, and Future

The world we know is no longer predictable, static, or steady. Changes are happening at a much faster speed, and the consequences and influences are becoming ever-more permanent. To fully understand where HR as an industry is going, we must first understand its past evolution and where we are heading.

An entire book can be dedicated to the history of HR transformation. To set the scene for our discussions, what follows is a brief recap of how HR has changed over the centuries as the economy has changed and how different levels of market maturity align with differing HR maturity. This recap is helpful because it serves as a reminder of how the HR function has evolved while recognising that some of the early influences and perceptions of the function remain in the contemporary workforce.

THE FIRST INDUSTRIAL REVOLUTION: HR AS EMPLOYER-ORIENTED ADMINISTRATORS

Occurring from the mid-eighteenth to early nineteenth centuries, the First Industrial Revolution is marked by our shift from a sole reliance on animals, human effort, and biomass as primary sources of energy to the use of fossil fuels to enable mechanical power. This period was the first transformation to an industrial economy from an agricultural one in certain areas of Europe and North America, starting in Great Britain and followed by Belgium, Germany, and France. Characteristics of this early industrialisation were technological progress, a shift from rural work to industrial labour, financial investments in new industrial structures, and early developments in class consciousness and theories related to it.

This period brought the notion of specialisation, courtesy of Karl Marx, to the forefront. This was the age of the factory. Factories needed workers to fill positions, man machinery, and churn out products and goods for the masses. Scientific management is a theory of management that analyses and synthesises workflows. Its main objective is improving economic efficiency, especially labour productivity. It was one of the earliest attempts to apply science to the engineering of processes and to management. One early approach to scientific management is known as Taylorism, after its founder Frederick W. Taylor, which was developed from a factory management system in the late nineteenth century to increase efficiency by breaking down production into specialised repetitive tasks.

This had enormous implications to HR. Evaluating every step in a manufacturing process and breaking it down to minimal tasks suggested that the workforce was largely replaceable with minimal dependencies. Thus, retention and employee wellness were not the focus for employers or HR, and most of the bandwidth was spent on ensuring production efficiencies.

HR in the time of the First Industrial Revolution was very much administrative in nature, as human capital was viewed as labour intensive and not knowledge-based. HR focused on recruitment and efficiency of the labour force. HR's role was to recruit and pay workers. HR jobs were seen as low-level administrative positions, and those in HR departments often reported to office managers. At this stage, the majority of Asian countries had not yet begun to conceptualise HR management as European countries led the way in this First Industrial Revolution.

THE SECOND INDUSTRIAL REVOLUTION: EMPLOYEE-ORIENTED HR

The Second Industrial Revolution occurred between the end of the nineteenth century and the first two decades of the twentieth century, and it brought major breakthroughs in electricity distribution, wireless and wired communication, and new forms of power generation. Soon came the refinement of the steam engine, the invention of the internal combustion engine, the harnessing of electricity, and the construction of canals, railways, and electric power lines. Employees of this era were not seen as a return on investment for a business; they were considered a cost.

The invention of the assembly line gave this phase a boost. Coal mines, steel mills, and textile factories were common places of work. There was an increased focus on management as well as health and safety in the workplace, given the rise of high-risk work environments, such as coal mines, along with the growing popularity of trade unions.

Post–World War II marks the next evolutionary period. We then saw HR shift into a space where it handled people challenges within the white collar working population. This point in history became pivotal for HR leaders as the conversation grew from just paying workers their wages to focusing on their well-being and how to drive productive teamwork. HR was tapped to do much of the heavy lifting on these issues.

HR's responsibilities grew from meeting payroll to finding ways to retain employees and keep them happy in their positions. "Happy employees and productive employees" was the most common sentiment during this period. HR became more aware of the human capital contribution through knowledge and innovation, but much of HR advancement was focused more on research than practice, especially on the links between motivation and productivity. Interest in organisational psychology and employee relations grew. During this period, HR was often interpreted as a compliance function that continued to carry most of the administrative and legislative burden.

THE FLUID THIRD INDUSTRIAL REVOLUTION: HR AS A BUSINESS PARTNER

The Third Industrial Revolution began in the 1950s with the development of digital systems, communication, and rapid advances in technology, which enabled new ways of generating, processing, and sharing information. Many mature markets find themselves in this phase of transformation today, with the strong belief that HR is an equal partner to the business. The chief HR officer now enjoys a seat next to the chief financial officer and contributes with other senior leaders within the business, helping to develop and grow the organisation.

HR is finally being given an opportunity to make a bigger impact on the business and being recognised for it. As world trade and globalisation become more complex, HR has the accountability and ability to help solve more sophisticated problems.

HR leaders seek to solve the problems of today and plan for tomorrow through responsibilities such as performance management and succession planning.

What is significant during this phase is the popularisation of the Ulrich HR business partner model, wherein HR competencies are articulated to show the complexity and evolution of HR. Research in HR becomes more complex and critical, focusing on challenging issues, such as leadership and culture. We will discuss Ulrich's research and perspectives in greater detail shortly.

During this period, HR leaders also saw the need to practise more organisational governance and began holding the stewardship of organisation policies and procedures. This is when best practices for HR began to gain momentum as HR, and companies as a whole, began to look to the practices, policies, and procedures that the large, very successful companies used. Most HR divisions at this time were structured under finance or operations, rather than as their own entities within a business.

HR in most emerging markets is still yet to fully evolve to this phase, given that the focus on corporate governance and baseline HR practices re-engineering is likely top of mind. Personnel departments are turning into HR departments, which then begin to manage processes and procedures around the globalised workforce. Most HR functions have started to run complex solutions, which make information about employees available to HR business leaders anywhere and anytime. We see more emerging markets practising and anchoring HR roles, especially as more and more emerging unicorns scale up, including GoJek in Indonesia and FoodPanda in Singapore.

By the end of the twentieth century, East Asia became one of the most recently industrialised regions of the world. The BRICS states (Brazil, Russia, India, China, and South Africa) began to undergo the process of industrialisation. Europe and the US continued to lead and mature as world leaders in globalisation and trade.

THE WAY OF THE FUTURE, THE FOURTH INDUSTRIALISATION: AGILE HR WITH A GROWTH MINDSET

The concept of the Fourth Industrial Revolution was coined in 2016 by World Economic Forum founder Klaus Schwab in a book of the same title. The Fourth Industrial Revolution can be described as the advancement and innovation of "cyber-physical systems," which give rise to entirely new capabilities for people and machines. While these capabilities are reliant on the technologies and infrastructure of the Third Industrial Revolution, the Fourth Industrial Revolution represents completely new ways in which technology becomes embedded within societies and even our human bodies. Technologies that will impact our fundamental understanding of the self—and our very existence—are being developed, including genome editing, new forms of machine intelligence, machine learning and algorithms, and cryptographic methods such as the blockchain.

The challenge for HR in the Fourth Industrial Revolution lies in the fluidity of needing to live out the vision of the Third Revolution's HR strategy while at the same time manoeuvring between the complex new organisational capability requirements and fundamental shifts in work brought about by the likes of the COVID-19 pandemic. HR leaders are now expected to be able to recruit new and unique skillsets like bitcoin technologists and be excited to provide recommendations that cater to the changing work dynamics. For instance, where physical team huddles have traditionally been utilised as one of the most effective ways to drive innovation, some 80 per cent of the workforce may now be working remotely on highly innovative projects during the pandemic.

As the Fourth Industrial Revolution is just rearing its head, the opportunity exists for the HR function to redefine the way of working and thinking proactively, in comparison to the earlier phases of industrialisation, in which HR evolution may have been more reactive. This could redefine the way forward for HR.

✳ ✳ ✳

The way forward is developing a growth mindset—and celebrating the death of best practices.

Dave Ulrich, a renowned HR researcher and professor, shared

his observations, reflections, and explorations as 2021 kicked off amidst the global pandemic. Ulrich called out the fact that benchmarking and best practices have been integral to the development of the HR function and have a long history in shaping the profession. Many thoughtful HR leaders continue to propose reinventing HR practices through benchmarking and best practices.

Ulrich suggested there are merits to such a perspective, as benchmarking can serve as the baseline to report on what HR is doing against a standard (which could be global, industry-based, or historical) to build on strengths or to identify areas that require further development. Best practices, meanwhile, can lead followers to success by learning from others.

Ulrich called for a future that is in close alignment with the thesis of this book, wherein HR leaders pivot from benchmarking and best practices to focusing on providing *guidance*. Ulrich suggested that instead of attempting to improve by comparing to benchmarks and by adapting what others do well through best practices, we must move beyond these and towards a much more proactive approach of *prescriptions*. Ulrich introduced the idea that prescriptions will anticipate what should be done and focus on results. Prescriptions guide choices to deliver results through vested practices.

Ulrich outlined clear steps for the HR function to pivot and to continuously challenge best practices. I have included these steps in this chapter, as the strategies are particularly useful to consider at the HR functional and team level. This book, however, will focus more on individual growth mindset shifts and practices for its remainder.

Step 1: Define desired results. Ulrich reminds us that the HR function centres on supporting five stakeholder groups and themes in receiving the outcomes that matter to them: employee, strategy, customer, investor, and community. Defining the stakeholder and what matters in your context is extremely useful in aligning organisational initiatives towards those results.

Step 2: Classify human capital initiatives. There are thousands of human capital initiatives that are made up of various processes, practices, or interventions. Ulrich has classified these complex ideas into four human capital categories and identified a total of thirty-six initiatives in each pathway: talent, leadership, organisation, and human resources. These four pathways and thirty-six initiatives capture the breadth of human capital development and the enormous opportunities that can be unlocked through the HR function.

Step 3: Measure human capital initiatives. Each of the human capital initiatives can be measured several different ways and in a 360-degree manner. For example, surveys can be used to measure the perception of employees within the organisation, or indicators from organisational data, like productivity, can be measured by revenue or profit per employee.

Step 4: Determine which human capital initiatives deliver desired results. Each of the human capital initiatives impacts each of the five stakeholder results differently. The impact can provide guidance about where to invest in human capital to deliver the outcomes that matter. In summary, Ulrich and his colleagues have suggested algorithms that determine which of the thirty-six human capital initiatives impact each of the five stakeholder results. It is definitely worth reading up on if you are interested in diving into this at a more functional level.

Step 5: Invest in the human capital initiatives that matter most. Once the prioritised human capital initiatives are identified, the organisation can focus on what matters rather than blindly following or pursuing best practices. The organisational resources should be directed to tailored initiative innovation and improvement to achieve outcomes that are meaningful for the organisation.

Step 6: Monitor the impact of the human capital investments on results over time. Ulrich issues a great reminder that HR initiatives and impact assessments must be understood through a longitudinal lens and not in a single event or snapshot view.

These six steps outlined by Ulrich all require a fundamental pivot away from focusing on benchmarking and best practices. Ulrich envisions a future in which any business or HR leader talking about human capital will be much less focused on discussing what others do and replicating them, and instead more committed and informed about what they can do within their own organisations to achieve their specific desired outcomes.

* * *

THE BRAVE NEW WORLD FOR HR: HR PHILOSOPHIES AND HR OPERATING MODELS

HR leaders continue to struggle with an aligned core value proposition, as HR means very different things to different stakeholders. Many business leaders do not fully comprehend the value that HR brings to the organisation and often assume simplicity in the capabilities required to perform core functions, such as recruitment, payroll, and people-related governance. The ability for HR leaders to articulate our core values without using the broad-brush term "strategic" becomes a critical path to an impactful partnership. I want to provide clarity on two often misunderstood or misinterpreted concepts: *HR philosophies* and *HR operating models*.

HR PHILOSOPHY: THE WAY WE *THINK* AND *MAKE* DECISIONS

When we ask HR leaders what their company's HR philosophy is, or what their personal HR philosophy is, we are often met with blank stares. Not because they do not care enough to have an answer, but because HR leaders often do not have the headspace or time to reflect on these questions.

At the organisational level, the HR philosophy addresses the intrinsic stance on which HR as a function bases its solutions. It provides consistency in approaches to baseline practices and how companies set boundaries for their employees. A robust HR philosophy reflects the company's values and the culture it aspires to have, and sets the standards for organisational process and initiative design. The clarity of the HR philosophy is also used as a way for organisations to brand and attract talent.

It is, therefore, not surprising to observe HR philosophies aligning with organisational values and products. For instance, a company that encourages innovation and collaboration may have an HR philosophy that is crafted more towards facilitating innovation and collaboration, which may then translate to flexibility in working hours with strong utilisation of virtual collaboration technologies. Similarly, many startups value treating employees as adults with common sense and honesty, which may translate to HR practices such as unlimited time off and no budget for travel, as is observed in technology giants such as Google, Netflix, and Riot Games in the early days of company formation.

Some useful dimensions to think through as you are articulating your organisational HR philosophy include:

- *What are our organisational values?*
- *What does high performance look like?*
- *What are the behaviours that we do not want to endorse?*
- *What do our companies' compensation and benefits say about us?*
- *Are our HR policies and processes aligned with our organisational HR philosophy?*

Some useful questions to ask yourself include:

- *How do I see the role of HR?*
- *What type of HR leader do I aspire to be?*
- *What experiences do I want the leaders and teams to have in their interactions with me?*
- *What part of my current environment do I struggle with when practising HR?*
- *What are my non-negotiables when I am designing HR solution recommendations?*

On an individual level, an HR philosophy provides guidance and guardrails on how HR leaders make recommendations and articulate the design of solutions. It is also your guiding North Star when you are assessing for organisational fit in alignment with your HR practices.

For instance, my philosophy of continuously challenging the status quo and moving away from best practices may not be aligned with an organisation that leans towards a more conservative and controlled style of culture and management.

There is no inherent right or wrong HR philosophy. It is about alignment and clarity in articulation.

HR OPERATING MODEL: THE WAY WE *DO* THINGS

Conceptually, the HR operating model addresses how headcount resources will be allocated and, to a certain extent, determines the employee and manager experiences. Most importantly, it determines the accountabilities of HR as a function as well as within the function. It allows the allocation of accountabilities and is often designed with scale and organisational maturity in mind. The HR operating model will drive the capability requirements of the HR team and, ultimately, influence the organisation's interaction and experiences of HR and understanding its relevant accountabilities.

The HR operating model and its ways of work will also be influenced by the organisation's decision around the level of centralisation. The organisation will provide the framework for where decisions are made and the realistic level of integration and influences of the HR leaders.

As HR evolves as a function, HR operating models continue

to evolve and coexist. Understanding the complexities of the different models can help us see more clearly where and how we must evolve. Note that this section of the book summarises the key trends and common models without value judgements. I will not suggest which is the best model or which is superior to another but will recognise that each model brings value to the organisation differently. It is important to clarify that the industrial revolution view shows the perceptions of HR from the outside, whereas the HR operation view illustrates the structural and practical ways that HR works within organisations and is accountable within such structures.

I deliberately separated the concepts of HR philosophy and HR operating model because they are not synonymous. There are various HR operating models, and they may or may not reflect on the maturity of the organisation's model and philosophy. Below, I outline some of the most popular operating models within organisations.

Model 1: Support Function Model

This was the most common operating model in the earlier industrial revolutions and in the early lifecycle of organisations, but the support function operating model is still very much alive and well.

HR reporting to the chief operating officer (COO) or chief financial officer (CFO) is a common manifestation of this operation model. The central role of this model assumes the supportive nature of HR, either under an operations or finance purview. The assumption of this model is that there is no strong, independent, strategic value within HR and that HR should implement the directions of the COO or CFO. Under this model, people are often considered a cost rather than a value.

This model is not unique to small enterprises, and it is still possible to observe this model in large contemporary organisations, though it does not necessarily represent the success of its HR function.

Model 2: HR Business Partner Model (the Ulrich Model)

HR as a partner to the business was popularised by Ulrich almost two decades ago. Ulrich is well known in the HR community for his advocacy of the HR businessperson role, also known as the "Ulrich model." It has been eighteen years since Ulrich published his classic book on human resource management, *Human Resource Champions*. In his book, he argues that HR is a triangle, and within that triangle sit three core positions and responsibilities: HR shared services are the core scalable administration function; a specialist group focuses on key talent functions, such as learning and development or compensation and benefits; and a generalist group acts as the business partner. Notably, the only internal stakeholder/client visible role in the Ulrich model is the HR business partner (HRBP).

The idea is that the HRBP will funnel through the needs of the business and use the other two anchors as support to deliver the outcome. The specialist will know very specialised advice, and the HR shared services, or the administration function, will provide seamless support to execute. The Ulrich model is intended to elaborate on the role of the HR business partner, advocating for HR to be business partners with influence equal to the other areas of the business, and lay out the key skills needed to fulfil that partnership. A generation of HR leaders have used the Ulrich model as the basis for transforming their HR functions, so in many mature market companies, you will see HR policy making, administration, and business partner roles separated.

In some ways, it has become a best practice for HR functions. The majority of global multinational companies (MNCs) will likely have an HR function that is operating in this structure, with varying degrees of success depending on the complexity and maturity of the organisation.

Model 3: Internal Consultancy/Agile Capacity-
Based Model (The McKenzie CHRO Model)

This model could be articulated and understood as an extension of the Ulrich model. To provide this sort of structural support without significantly increasing resource requirements, some HR functions have moved into much more agile and pool-based structures, leveraging technology more effectively. In this model, the triangle remains but with a more compact team of specialists and HRBPs. The key to this model is that there is a bigger pool of strong generalists to be mobilised to execute various projects and initiatives as needed. This operating model can only realise its full potential with strong HR capability and agility, which means the teams of generalists must be highly competent.

This model could be a great way to structure HR teams in emerging markets or hyper-growth organisations given that rapid changes in organisational priorities often require HR to respond quickly to high-impact needs of the business. However, this is probably the model that requires the highest degree of HR capabilities, and many emerging markets and hyper-growth companies struggle to build such HR capabilities to fully operate in it. Such contradiction is what makes this model almost too aspirational for most.

* * *

In some cases, an organisation's HR team may manifest in a mixture of the models. For instance, an enormously successful video games company with more than 3,000 employees globally operates with the combination of models 1 and 2, where the HR function reports to a head of enterprise (similar to a COO), and the HR teams operate in model 2 with business partners, the specialist talent function, and shared services clearly built out and defined.

BRINGING HR PHILOSOPHIES AND THE HR OPERATING MODEL TOGETHER

If we imagine an organisation as a human being, the operating model will be the skeleton and physical being of a human, while the philosophy will be the brain, heart, and soul. The misalignment of the two is often what causes stress and inefficiencies. Before thinking about growth-minded HR, I challenge you to think about your own HR philosophies and the HR operating model you or your organisation operate in.

- What are some of your organisational and personal challenges in HR?
- How many of those challenges are due to HR philosophical misalignment?

- How many are due to structural inefficiencies in the current operating model?
- What can you influence and change?
- What can you not influence and change?

In essence, you can apply the same HR philosophies to different HR operating models, and the outcomes will vary depending on the capabilities and philosophical commitment of the individuals involved. Having a sufficient understanding of the two and their parallel evolution is critical because it informs your choices and decisions on which operating model you want and can be effective in, as well as your philosophical stance as an HR leader.

This reflection is important in the context of growth-minded HR, as your operating environment will also determine the type of accountability and complex issues you must solve as an HR leader, which may in turn foster a different environment for you to practise the growth mindset.

CHAPTER 2

Moving from Best Practices to Growth Practices

I was a nervous wreck!

It was my first week as the head of HR transformation, and I was meeting the founder of one of the biggest scale-ups in Southeast Asia. I wanted to make an impression. Not just a positive impression but one that lets him know that I could be trusted with developing the people and culture framework that would inevitably lead the company to a historic initial public offering in 2022.

He waltzed into the room with a flare of self-confidence befitting a young founder who had appeared in *Forbes'* "30 Under 30" list in 2016 and *Fortune Indonesia*'s "40 Under 40" list in 2022.

As we talked about the challenges of designing a meaningful

career architecture for our technology teams, he looked me dead in the eye and asked, calmly and matter-of-factly, "What does Google do? What is the best practice?"

I froze. Not because I did not have an answer to his question, but because it gave me the uneasy signal of the challenges to come.

* * *

How often do you ask yourself, "What is the best practice?" when an HR issue arises? It may be in the context of organisational design or talent management or in regard to operational challenges faced when entering new markets.

Regardless, the answer may be: more often than you would like to admit.

This book is about the continuous journey of HR transformation and, more specifically, becoming a more growth-minded HR leader. To such ends, I call for us to ditch comfortable vocabularies around "best practices" and examine how we may approach HR issues with growth mindsets. We do not need to reinvent the wheel, but we do need to examine existing best practices critically and take a structured approach in reconsidering HR challenges.

WHAT ARE BEST PRACTICES?

Best practices were all the rage in the early 2000s. According to *Webster's New Millennium Dictionary of English*, best practices are defined as "practices which are most appropriate under the circumstances, especially as considered acceptable or regulated in business; techniques or methodologies that, through experience and research, have reliably led to desired or optimum results." This definition seems to fall short on mentioning innovation and creativity, with words such as "acceptable" and "reliable" anchoring this definition.

In HR, best practices are often derived through systematic and careful reflection on successful practical experience. Many rely on singular case studies or anecdotal stories to support the best-case assertions. We often like to focus on best practices as a collection of processes and procedures to be followed whenever a specific challenge arises. This understanding is partly true. Best practices in HR are built around what we would normally do in a situation, like how we could use the internet to recruit talent or the purpose of an internship program or a typical key organisational performance indicator via retention scores.

In other words, best practices seek to provide the answer without digging deeper into the root of the problem or desired impact.

There is no denying that HR best practices are a part of the business world—and for good reason. Type "HR best practices" into a Google search, and you will see more than 736 million results appear in 0.61 seconds. As HR business leaders, we love to talk about the best practices that have worked in other organisations or in our previous organisations and adopt what has worked elsewhere into our new settings.

Why are we so in awe of best practices?

It is tempting to use best practices as an HR leader because, for one, it lends an air of credibility. It conveys the message that "I am informed," "I am experienced," and "I know what success looks like." It also offers comfort because someone else has already done it and achieved success. Essentially, it is a mind-set that somewhat minimises the risk of innovation and dilutes the accountability and complexity associated with innovation through deep thinking.

In HR contexts, best practices prove that a particular way of recruiting talent, engaging our workforce, or improving employee skills actually works. We all want to drive real, tangible results and to show our senior leaders that HR provides enormous value to the health, growth, and success of our organisations. Best practices give us a solid framework to articulate that success.

Best practices are typically based on what worked well for Americans (such as the Ford model of performance management) and European companies (such as the more positive role and strong influence of the union) in mature markets. The assumption with best practices is that every organisation—whether it is small, medium, or large—in every industry can implement the same practices and processes to achieve the same positive results. In some cases, this is true, like with issues concerning health and safety. Research indicates, for example, that certain best practices, such as the implementation of workplace health and safety programs, reduce workplace accidents and improve morale. Many of these practices are, in fact, universally relevant and can be carried from industry to industry and organisation to organisation within all markets. Whether in a factory or in an office complex, for example, employees should hold onto the railing every time they walk down the stairs. That is a best practice. It provides safety for everyone, regardless of the market, size of the organisation, or industry.

While best practices for health and safety have a universal application, universal best practices are much rarer than you might believe.

In fact, there is very little evidence to prove that best practices will actually generate the same results for all companies. More often than not, best practices lead to mediocre performance because they lack agile application across industries, organisation size, and markets. Too many variables exist within companies for best practices to be truly effective in the ways we hope and want them to be. Yet HR leaders still turn to them, in part because they see hugely successful companies like Google, General Electric (GE), or General Motors using them. The belief is that, if it worked for those large, successful companies, then it can work for any organisation, regardless of its size, market, or culture.

Many CEOs and senior business leaders make the assumption that best practices lead to guaranteed positive results. CEOs may aspire for their companies to become the next Google and try to emulate what Google does. "If those powerful companies are successful using these practices, then of course, it can work for us too" goes the thinking. Many leaders look to companies like Google, Facebook, Microsoft, or GE for what to implement in their own organisations like a rite of passage to organisational growth and success.

I like to tell leaders that reaching for best practices when addressing critical organisational issues feels like getting dressed for an important life event by looking into someone else's closet! We rarely do so in our personal lives, so why do we feel the need to do so in our professional approaches?

Rarely do we find that what has worked for powerful brands will work universally. It could be argued that the term "best practices" is not synonymous with "universal" but that best practices take a simple, singular lens.

The world is more complex than best practices allow for. Best practices do not consider differences in cultures, markets, countries, or even within companies and management practices and styles. Just because an organisation has adopted a best practice does not mean it is the right practice for every organisation or that it will generate the desired results in every situation. Best practices often focus on an HR practice and process to be implemented to realise specific results, such as using the performance curve made at GE as a best practice to drive a high-performing culture.

Best practices are not universal truths.

BEST PRACTICES ARE A MINDSET

Best practices are more than just the "what." They are also the "how."

When HR leaders use best practices religiously, they rarely achieve the results they hope for. Finding innovative solutions is the answer to many talent life cycle challenges, yet HR leaders still reach for a best practice to answer a problem. If their results are mediocre at best, why do they keep reaching for them?

At the core, best practices are a mindset—a way the HR leader sees and thinks about the world around them, the problems they encounter, and how they choose to respond to them. Many CEOs demanded to know "How does (insert a desirable competitor) do this?" as the first point of reference when discussing HR challenges and initiatives they are facing, meaning that many of us have been conditioned to reach for the best practice in any given situation.

Questions on best practices from key stakeholders like the CEO and executive team members mean that HR leaders have not always been given the opportunity to look objectively at a challenge, evaluate various options, and think critically or innovatively about sustainable solutions. Demanding best practices distracts HR leaders from paying enough attention to the root cause of the issues and forces them to focus on a one-time fix instead of providing sustainable solutions to an issue, which often may not be obvious.

I recall an instance when one of the unicorn startups I worked with was constantly struggling with their in-house travel booking and reimbursement process. It was too slow. The best practice mindset and solution was to outsource the travel-related administration or to hire more people to support the workload. Taking a growth mindset approach to the issue, however, means that we dive deeper into the root cause of frequent travel by analysing travel data and patterns. Doing just that ultimately uncovered issues around the inconsistent travel policies between different job levels, which resulted in confusion and the inability to scale the administration. The way in which the international expansion team was structured also meant that the travel requirements were not sustainable for the growth trajectories of the region. The recommendation here was to review the travel policies and the international expansion team's structural accountabilities rather than purely addressing the speed of reimbursements and resource commitment of the travel administration team.

Having a solution-focused—but not quick-fix-oriented—growth mindset means that we need to understand each challenge with a fresh pair of eyes and ears, and use best practices only as a reference framework for solutions under consideration.

WHAT ARE GROWTH PRACTICES?

Shifting away from the best practice mindset allows us to look for growth practices.

"Growth" in Latin is *incrementum*. I like the way it frames growth as something incremental and not leapfrog. Incremental growth allows us the time to reflect and learn and continue to reframe our approach to issues.

Growth practices challenge the status quo and current narratives.

I would like to encourage us to use and consider the term "practice" in a multifaceted way. It may be used as a way for us to describe and connect with the customary, habitual, or expected procedure or way of doing something—as we use it in the term "best practices." But we can also use it as a way to describe how we may perform an activity or exercise a skill regularly to acquire, improve, or maintain proficiency in it—such as practising a growth mindset approach to deriving HR solutions. It is similar to how we talk about yoga practices or swimming practices.

"Growth practice" takes on the spirit of a growth mindset when thinking about what we do and how we do it.

A growth practice has five characteristics:

1. It challenges current thinking without simply repackaging the same narratives.
2. It makes people feel uncomfortable. It may be perceived as the "wrong" way of doing or thinking but with no evidence to validate those claims.
3. It is not always driven by quantitative "use cases."
4. It is outward looking rather than inward looking.
5. It is not a perfect solution and should not become a best practice. It is a practice that can continue to evolve and build on its own gaps.

Similar to best practices, growth practices could also be understood as a mindset—a growth mindset approach to issues and challenges. A mindset that is open and curious about the possibilities for solving people-related issues in ways that may not have been approached before.

Growth-minded HR thinks about sustainable solutions beyond the organisation we operate in. One of the core anchors for a growth-minded HR is the ability to connect the dots across the industry, organisation, team, and individuals and translate that connection into impactful solutions.

* * *

Best practices promote mediocre results at best. How can we reimagine a world of growth practices through our current best practices?

HR leaders have been conditioned to believe that when a situation arises, they must look to the best practice, implement it, and await a victorious and glorious outcome. The reality is anything but. We, who are invested and committed to best practices, are often left with mediocre results that never truly resolve the issues that the organisation wants to solve. Nor are we able to showcase the transformative potential of the HR function.

Below are some best practices case studies I have observed that are still deeply rooted in many organisations and may derail our efforts to build an agile and resilient workforce in this ever-changing landscape. I offer some reflective inquiry questions to think about how you can approach these scenarios differently and build growth practices. We will also dive into what I call "WOW practices," which give a *wow* with exclamation marks when introduced and that often becomes the aspirational best practice that many organisations strive for without adapting for the context of their organisation.

BEST PRACTICE CASE STUDY 1: HIGH RETENTION IS AN INDICATOR OF ORGANISATIONAL SUCCESS

When we are asked to measure the success of an organisation's HR efforts, what do we do? Most likely, we look at how long team members stay in their positions and/or at the organisation.

Many organisations continue to have an HR matrix that looks at turnover with the belief that the smaller that number is, the better. Perhaps even more concerning, most organisations use the retention number as an indicator of HR success.

Is the length of time someone stays in a position or at an organisation really the best measurement of success?

It does not account for the changing climate of the organisation, nor does it reflect on its leadership. In an emerging market or hyper-growth technology startup context, HR leaders with a growth mindset may look to high retention as an indication of HR challenges rather than something to be celebrated. Sometimes, the best thing for an employee, an organisation, or the market is for people to move on from one organisation to the next.

I imagine a future in which we acknowledge that a best-practice-informed fixed mindset is inward looking. A fixed mindset is about asking what benefits one's own organisation and *only* one's own organisation—rather than a growth-minded consideration on what could benefit the industry as a whole or the potential contribution to market transformation. Therefore, if we go back to the original question of an organisation's retention program as the measurement of success, growth practitioners should focus more on the retention of knowledge and building a mechanism that allows the sharing of knowledge rather than the retention of actual employees.

How can we reframe HR success away from the retention of employees to the retention (or even creation) of knowledge?

Growth-minded HR looks to learn and share learning, and to amplify the benefits of such learning into the broader society.

To move away from the best practice mindset is to start thinking about the ecosystem that we and the organisation operate in. Given that much of the growth mindset is centred around learning, the concept of learning must be built into the fabric of HR solutions because the responsibility of growing a country's talent pool—and thus its market—is as much an organisation's as it is the government's.

BEST PRACTICE CASE STUDY 2: FORCED PERFORMANCE RATING RANKING FOR MAINTAINING A STRONG PERFORMANCE CULTURE

The forced-ranking system is a common practice used for annual employee performance reviews in mature US and European markets. The assumption has been that every organisation—whether big, small, or merging with another—thrives in a high-performing culture, and the only way to achieve a high-performing culture is to use a forced-ranking bell curve to drive competition and motivate employees to succeed.

This practice was adopted and gained widespread popularity in the 1980s after General Electric's then-chief executive, Jack Welch, brought the ranking system to the organisation. In this system, employees are ranked from top to bottom, regardless of merit. There are the top 10 per cent performers, the bottom 10 per cent, and the other 80 per cent who fall in the middle (this formula is referred to as 10/80/10). For example, if you have a five-person team, one person would be at the top, one person at the bottom, and the other three would fall in the middle.

There is no deviation—regardless of talent. The forced-ranking system assumes there will always be a rational and logical statistical distribution for performance. Since it was first introduced, numerous companies have brought the practice in-house, each to varying degrees of success. Microsoft has been known to use the "best practice of bell curve performance management" as an example of pitting employees against one another so the organisation can reward the excellent and weed out the weak.

Does forced ranking really achieve the result of creating a high-performance culture for every organisation?

How can we reimagine performance management growth practices?

Not every organisation agrees forced ranking is a best practice. Accenture, a global management consultancy, for example, is pioneering changes in performance reviews. In 2015, the organisation moved away from forced ranking to "individualised performance," choosing to look at an individual's strengths and weaknesses. Accenture's CEO at the time, the late Pierre Nanterme, who spent thirty-two years working for the organisation, explained the move this way: "If there is something I am fighting against every day, it is conservatism. Status quo. When I ask the question, 'Why are we doing what we are doing?' if I receive the answer, 'This is the way we have always been doing it,' it drives me nuts. This is what we as leaders need to fight against, especially in large organisations."

Despite the questionable effectiveness of forced ranking, many companies continue to adopt the same approach to employee performance reviews. I have observed this in mature MNCs and emerging growth startups.

But ranking on a curve often does not translate. It either does not represent the makeup of an organisation's talent and business maturity, or it becomes a performance culture guide within the organisation. I have observed that in high-performing organisations, the forced ranking induces a sense of unfairness. When people are judged by the "worst of the best" mentality, it sometimes translates to a culture of counterproductive competitiveness. In more emerging organisations, it also does not reflect the fluid nature of roles and the talent population recruited in startup environments.

What does throwing all the curves away look like?

How can we manage and assess performance based on what our teams look like?

How can we maintain an individualised performance framework that uses more one-on-one performance reviews that allow us to measure employees' growth and evolution on an individual, rather than a comparative, basis?

BEST PRACTICE CASE STUDY 3: HIRING FROM JOB DESCRIPTIONS FOR THE BEST FIT

The Society for Human Resource Management (SHRM), based in the United States, continues to advocate for the best practices of writing a job description (JD). Just to be clear, I absolutely agree that there is still a place in the world for a JD. It can serve as an important and useful function for candidates, employees, and organisations. A clear JD typically covers the realistic title of the role, the expected tasks of the role, the key stakeholder that one will interact with, the necessary skills and competencies, and the organisation's culture. All of those things put together are key to presenting an open role to the market and letting candidates know how they will be assessed. In many cases, JDs may also serve as follow-up documents for performance review and management.

The best practice of a solid JD as the point of entry into an organisation may become problematic, however, because the market shifts so rapidly that businesses must constantly change and roles must evolve. There is very little guarantee that the JD written today will look the same six months from now. In fact, it would likely look different. This is almost always the case since a one-pager, regardless of how well it is written, is likely unable to capture the complexity and expectations of jobs today.

To further reduce the effectiveness of this best practice approach, the skills and experiences that organisations base their hiring decisions on are built upon the tasks that one expects the role to perform as described in the JD. This best practice approach will likely miss the skillset one may possess that allows one to adapt for the future. Skills for the changing future, such as agility, resilience, or having a growth mindset, are much less prevalent in JDs. We must work to identify ways in which we can assess and identify these skillsets in potential candidates.

Tapping into growth practice potential, I would love to reimagine the job description and reshape the way we communicate with future candidates.

How are JDs limiting your organisation or talent's success?

What could be an alternative to a JD?

A growth practice may look like a job impact (JI) statement

instead of a JD. Instead of focusing on creating the right job description and hiring based on keywords and skills, we focus on describing the impact the work is achieving, regardless of the changing context and environment. We also need to accept that roles evolve, which no JD will capture.

What could this growth practice look like when hiring, say, a recruiter? This will shift our perspective and dialogues. A recruiter's typical job description may state that one of the tasks and requirements is to fill all required positions with a Service Level Agreement (SLA) of three months. This will likely direct the search to find someone who has a track record in recruitment with similar SLAs, but it also communicates the performance expectations from SLAs only. A JI statement for a recruiter may emphasise the impact of bringing the best talent into the company to deliver on the organisation's vision. This will mean that the candidate's expectation is not about filling roles in three months as the success indicator. Instead, success could take six months, but the roles are filled with high-impact employees with critical skills who are difficult to find but that can truly deliver innovative business outcomes.

By focusing on communicating to candidates why the role is important to the organisation's short- and long-term strategies, we can then discuss how the candidate might apply their unique skills to the position. As a result, HR and business leaders can evaluate the potential hire against the impact needed for the organisation and focus discussions on the changing needs of the organisation as a reality assessment.

A growth-minded HR leader will understand the need to find candidates who can meet immediate needs *and* who have the ability to evolve their contributions and skills as the business evolves. Creating a JI statement requires the HR leader to work closely with other business leaders in thinking beyond the primary concern of surviving the day or week and instead looking into mid- to long-term planning for organisational success.

What could other growth practices for recruitment using a JI statement look like?

BEST PRACTICE CASE STUDY 4: BEHAVIOUR AND PAST SUCCESS INTERVIEW QUESTIONS AS THE PREDICTOR OF CANDIDATE SUCCESS

JD best practices have also shaped the way we think about interviews and candidate selection. With the growth practice of JI statements, there is also the need to change the interview conversation.

Behaviour and past success interview questions have long been considered the predictor of candidate success. HR and business leaders tend to focus on what a candidate has done in previous positions and what they did to solve certain problems in the past and the outcomes. The assumption that the past informs the present calls for candidates to regurgitate previous ways of approaching a problem rather than thinking about the future and the contexts that are unique to each organisation.

"Give me an example when you have successfully solved a conflict" is an example of a best-practice-informed interview question that is commonly used in interviews. But the indication of how well someone solved a problem in the past does not always translate to how well they can engage with a current problem. Further complicating the validity of such an approach, questions that are based on showcasing success are inherently self-biased.

What could asking for examples of failures look like?

What could asking for solving real problems with current evolving contexts look like?

Asking questions that dive into potential employees' growth mindset and their innate ability to solve future problems could be a more accurate indicator of potential role fit. We are hiring employees to solve the problems of today and tomorrow, not yesterday. This is a distinct shift in mindset—from thinking about the tasks to be done and responsibilities to be fulfilled to thinking instead about the impact we want new hires to make.

When the focus is on impact, the conversation suddenly shifts to what problems need solving. This growth practice means we need to be asking questions that are much more directed towards "Walk me through how you would solve this case," rather than "Tell me about a time you resolved a dispute between a manager and their team." We need to encourage sharing thought processes rather than simply talking through what a candidate has done in the past under similar circumstances.

This also requires a mindset shift from business and HR leaders, where we are not looking for the right answers but are looking for the right approach and consideration as part of a bigger problem-solving framework that one gravitates towards. A growth mindset approach means that, to a large extent, a candidate's answer does not matter as much as their ability and thought process when they attempt to solve the problem. In this approach, you are able to experience how a candidate critically thinks while evaluating whether they can think quickly and innovatively (i.e., outside of the best practice mindset). In this way, we sneak a peek into their potential.

Our world is changing so quickly, and we must respond with agility.

We are solving the problems of tomorrow today, so how can we ask interview questions that give us a peek into the future rather than the past?

BEST PRACTICE CASE STUDY 5: CONDUCTING EXIT INTERVIEWS FOR ORGANISATIONAL IMPROVEMENTS

Exit interviews have long been a traditional tool to identify the areas where organisations can improve to retain their talent. It typically looks like an anonymous feedback form or some kind of interview with an HR representative when employees have resigned, often in their last few days of employment. We typically see an attempt to aggregate the data from various exiters and to derive insights and provide potential improvement initiatives that usually assume an organisational-wide initiative.

Exit interviews often provide limited insights because they are either constrained to the individual situation (e.g., a new mother wants to spend more time with her baby) or subjective experiences (e.g., not getting promoted). Many employees may not want to burn bridges before they leave, or, given that they have already made the decision to leave, they may share limited truth during this meeting or survey. In larger organisations, these meetings are sometimes conducted by assigned HR personnel who may not have a close relationship with the existing employee, making the exit interview an onerous and transactional process that yields very limited success.

Reimagining exit interviews within a growth mindset may mean that the exit interview as a concept no longer exists. Instead of asking talent why they leave when they leave, we want to know what makes them stay and continue to show up to work.

What insights could stay interviews bring for you and the organisation that an exit interview cannot?

By having regular conversions with employees (above and beyond the large-scale employee engagement surveys), insights may be shared that are timely for organisational change and development. Reimagining stay interviews as a practice that is not initiated and owned by HR but as one that is integrated in employee lifecycle processes (i.e., stay interviews during the performance management cycle) will help us to reframe the accountabilities of people managers. Reimagining a growth approach that is advocated for and conducted by people managers in partnership with HR when it comes to analysis and action planning could be a game changer.

These "stay interviews," as we might call them as the opposite of the "exit interview," will enable a two-way conversation in real time, rather than after the fact, and provide a space and time for employees to ask questions and shape the conversation. Stay interviews may not be a novel idea, but the continued practice of exit interviews suggests that many of us are still not ready to move beyond best practices and the mindset associated with them.

Growth practices are about changing mindsets.

∗ ∗ ∗

BEST PRACTICE VERSUS "THE WOW PRACTICE"

In addition to best practices, I want to dive into what I call "WOW practices," as we often find it challenging to decouple the two types of practices. It is not uncommon for leaders to perceive and embrace WOW practices as best practices without a deeper understanding and analysis of the contextual fit of the practice to the market, industry, and organisation. WOW practices are usually innovative when first introduced and are often investment-intensive, with shining bells and whistles that divert attention away from the potential dark sides associated with implementation.

WOW PRACTICE CASE STUDY 1: ORGANISATION-WIDE FREE MEALS FOR ALL (CHANNELLING GOOGLE AND FACEBOOK [NOW META], THE OH-SO SILICON VALLEY PRACTICE)

Google is known as one of the best companies to work for. It has a culture that is the envy of many workers and companies. One practice that both Google and Facebook use is providing free meals to their employees. It appears that Maslow's hierarchy of needs may have served as a framework for HR practices with the operating assumption that, if they take care of employees' basic needs for food, water, and shelter, employees will focus more on achieving the next level of enlightenment in their work.

The meals are not just free; the food is notably restaurant quality, with buffet options of international cuisines to serve employees on one dedicated floor. I remember visiting one of my previous colleagues at the Singapore Facebook headquarters (HQ) and was led to one of these cafes, where I got to choose from fifteen flavours of ice cream with gummy bear toppings as a treat. I finally understood why my colleague did not bother to step outside of his office building for our meeting! Free meals may be a WOW, but they may also cost upward of $4 million annually to make happen. Financial considerations aside, some sceptics have suggested the free meal strategy ultimately squeezes more out of the employees as they stay in the office for longer on average.

What is interesting is that, at the time of this writing, as we hope to be at the tail-end of the COVID-19 pandemic, Google has decided to scrap its famous, lavish staff buffets as it reopens its offices, but employees can still get free food in the form of lunch boxes and snacks. Google has stated that since they are offering a hybrid office model post-pandemic, this has prompted them to rethink their facilities and employee perks strategies. The fact that a WOW practice originator has since abandoned the practice prompts an interesting reflection on how sustainable WOW practices truly are.

Channelling a growth mindset, here are some reflective questions to consider before you adopt or design a WOW practice:

- *What is the problem we are trying to solve with WOW practices?*
- *What could be the dark side to a WOW practice?*
- *Are WOW practices sustainable?*
- *What does rolling back such WOW practices mean for the future?*

WOW PRACTICE CASE STUDY 2: PAY EMPLOYEES TO LEAVE DURING PROBATION (CHANNELLING ZAPPOS AND RIOT GAMES)

Zappos is well known for pioneering the concept of maintaining a productive and satisfied workforce by paying unmotivated new employees to leave. The Zappos theory is that it weeds out people who are not a fit for the organisation early. If someone is willing to accept a buy-out, then they would never have lasted long at the organisation. Similar approaches are being adopted by high-growth companies like Riot Games, where they pay a generous percentage of an employee's base salary to encourage them to "exit the game" early.

I recall once having the CEO of a low-performing startup demand to apply the Zappos best practice of paying employees $2,000 to quit after they had completed their four-week training as a way to rectify the current under-performance. In this situation, the CEO was desperate to improve retention and performance issues. He also faced challenges in the organisation's brand, which was not attracting the type of employees he wished to attract and retain. There is a high chance that, by introducing the WOW practice, some of the longstanding and productive employees would perceive it to be an unfair and fiscally irresponsible practice because the average salary for the company was about $400 a month.

The CEO was more enthralled with the *wow* factor of paying employees to quit. He thought it would attract the right people by building a different brand for the startup, even though it was still in its early stages of development and had limited funding. The CEO became enamoured with the practice more than he was with finding the right solution to the recruitment, retention, and performance challenges. He was more interested in using it as an employee branding strategy than focusing on the problem that we needed to solve together.

Channelling a growth mindset, here are some reflective questions with this specific WOW practice in mind:

- *What would a growth practice for selection and retention look like?*
- *Is this a WOW practice that simply repackages future redundancies or takes away the burden of future performance improvement plan (PIP) processes?*
  - *Is the PIP a best practice that is no longer as effective as it is intended to be?*
- *What is the darker side of this practice for current employees?*

WOW PRACTICE CASE STUDY 3: NO FORMAL PERFORMANCE REVIEW AND NO PIP FOR LOW PERFORMERS (CHANNELLING NETFLIX)

Netflix has pioneered many WOW practices, which their previous executives Reed Hastings and Erin Meyer shared in the popular 2020 book titled *No Rules Rule: Netflix and the Culture of Reinvention*. Netflix has probably been cited more often than Google in the past five years as having an aspirational culture. I have been asked, "How can we encourage a culture like Netflix?" too often to count.

I was in awe of the *Harvard Business Review* article in which the previous chief HR officer of Netflix, Patty McCord, shared the pioneering WOW HR practices at Netflix. One of them was paying top of the market and having a high guaranteed bonus, with a philosophy of "telling the truth about performance."

Netflix eliminated formal reviews many years ago upon the realisation that they were too ritualistic and too infrequent. Netflix believed that building a bureaucracy and elaborate rituals around measuring performance usually does not improve it. Instead, managers and employees are expected to have conversations about performance as an organic part of their work.

Traditional corporate performance reviews and performance improvement plans are driven largely by fear of litigation. Organisations can be loath to let go of low performers without documented attempts to improve. This is somewhat masked under best practices and a utopian idea of supporting employee development. Instead, Netflix practices telling the truth about role and performance, which is then supported by generous exit packages.

This WOW practice is further supported by the talent strategy of no variable performance bonuses. A top-of-the-market base salary with an embedded fixed bonus assumes that *everyone* is a high performer—or you do not belong there. The darker side of this WOW practice potentially means that much of HR's time is spent managing the aftermath of those *not* perceived as high performers and their departures.

What remains to be seen is how this WOW practice, with its "perform or get out" mentality, truly influences the performance culture in the long run. What we do know is that, at the time of this writing, the pandemic has rattled the way of work worldwide. Netflix was forced to lay off about 5 per cent of its workforce in mid-2022 to overhaul its business strategies. This indicated that even an investment-intensive WOW practice that supposedly attracted and retained only the best talent did not translate to optimal business outcomes that secured the financial sustainability of Netflix.

Channelling a growth mindset, here are some reflective questions with this specific WOW practice in mind:

- *Where do we find the balance between variable and fixed performance rewards?*
- *How do reward strategies drive performance culture and impact the role of HR?*
- *How does this shift the employee rewards narrative around joint and team ownership?*
- *What could a growth practice for performance review and reward look like for the future workforce in the post-pandemic world?*

* * *

Some of these WOW practices start to carry a flair of best practices.

Asking "How can we be more like Google or Netflix?" is fundamentally dishonest and misleading. A more honest and meaningful question may be "*Why* do we want our culture to be like Netflix or Google?"

Think about the *outcome* you want. Think about the problem you are trying to solve.

If we are solving for employee engagement with the intended outcome of a more engaged employee, then the question we should ask is "How do we best engage our teams and leaders?"

Not "How do we engage our employees like (insert other company names)?"

To answer, "How do we best engage our teams and leaders?" requires us to explore more deeply with multidimensional questions:

- *What do highly engaged teams and leaders look like in our organisation?*
- *How do we articulate our culture?*
- *How are we living our culture, and where are the gaps?*
- *How is our culture influencing employee engagement?*
- *How do we want to help our employees become more engaged given our organisation's resources, money, time, and unique situation?*
- *How do we collect and validate employee sentiments?*

When we approach best practices as if they are golden rules, we do not often find the space to ask more questions. In turn, we rarely get the results we need to truly experience an impact and shift. When we move into a growth mindset and ask more thoughtful and intentional questions rather than accepting the first best practice that provides us an easy answer, we allow the answers to guide and lead us to design growth practices that are unique to the needs of our organisation.

* * *

HOW CAN HR TRANSFORM AS A FUNCTION?

We have examined the history of HR transformation and best practices that we have all likely embraced as an HR function at some point in our careers.

Ulrich, in his decades of HR research and advocacy, recently presented some compelling arguments about why best practices and benchmarks could be roadblocks to the future of strategic HR.

In early 2021, as we entered another year of the COVID-19 pandemic, Ulrich shared an article on LinkedIn titled "HR's Reinvention: Moving from Benchmarking and Best Practices to Guidance," in which he suggested that one of the problems of focusing on best practices is that they centre on others and not on oneself. The concept of comparing to and learning from others is essentially useful, but the primary agenda should be determining whether or not the human capital "best" practice will help your organisation meet its unique goals. The benchmark should not be others but yourself, and you should work towards personalised goals. We, as human beings, do not set out to become just like someone else and follow their life choices to a tee. Why should we expect to do that when making organisational choices?

Ulrich reminded us that best practices focus backwards more than forward. Learning what others have done will always leave you behind them as they reinvent. Too often, a best practice is considered in isolation and not within its entire context. Adapting only a piece of the overall system does not often transfer success to another setting. Fundamentally, best practices create circular thinking and do not promote innovation. Observing and learning from others often causes us to share existing ideas rather than create new ones.

Ulrich summarises the differences well below:

HR REINVENTION FROM BENCHMARKING
TO BEST PRACTICE TO GUIDANCE

	BENCHMARKING	BEST PRACTICE	GUIDANCE
Answers the Question:	How do I compare to others?	What are others doing that I can learn from?	What human capital initiatives should I invest in to deliver key results?
Starts with…	How am I doing?	What are others doing?	What should I be doing?
Improve through…	Build on strengths; overcome weaknesses	Learning and mimicking what others have done	Investing in initiatives that deliver results
Fundamental assumption	Description	Imitation	Prescription
Primary analytics tool	Dashboards/ Scorecards	Insights and interventions	Impact and outcomes
Breadth	Generally scores on single human capital area (talent, leadership, or organization)	Accesses others' practice in a specific human capital initiative	Evaluates which human capital area (talent, leadership, organization, HR) and initiative delivers results

Source: David, Ulrich, "HR's Reinvention: Moving from Benchmarking and Best Practices to Guidance," LinkedIn, January 12, 2021, https://www.linkedin.com/pulse/hrs-reinvention-moving-from-benchmarking-best-practices-dave-ulrich/.

I include the table here in support of Ulrich's continuous research and narrative around how HR as a function must move away from the point of transformation to the point of reinvention.

Sharing the same sentiment, in this book, we are reimagining HR.

Ulrich is advocating for HR leaders to pivot to a model of guidance, which is built on benchmarking as the baseline for how an organisation compares to others, and uses best practices as a bridge, highlighting the practices other organisations have successfully used. Guidance focuses on what should be done to deliver your organisation's results from human capital investments, with deep organisational context embedded as the point of reference and creativity.

With a vision shared with Ulrich, in this book, we will dive deeper into how individual HR leaders, with the optimism to become more curious and anchored within a growth mindset, can advocate for and facilitate this HR reimagination.

Progress comes from spiralling forward more than recycling the past.

PART II

Curiosity and Grit: Levers to Cultivate a Growth Mindset

In Part I of this book, we unpacked the continuous transformation journey that HR leaders are on, as well as called out why best practice is truly mediocre at best.

In Part II, I now invite you to shift gears and think about how we, as HR leaders, can cultivate a growth mindset through curiosity and grit as a foundation to help us break out from the comfort and safe zone of best practices.

* * *

One of the most interesting parts of my career has been interviewing talent. In the last fifteen years, conservatively, I have interviewed close to half a million people of varying seniority in various industries and companies. Every interview is like an adventure. You really do not know what you are going to get out of the meetings, regardless of how prepared you are or how well written a candidate's CV is.

"What do you look for in a candidate during the interview?" is probably one of the most frequently asked questions I hear.

I used to meet those curious and hopeful eyes with a long-winded description of capabilities ranging from communication to problem-solving. I used to think we look for great first impressions, which are often the result of excellent communication skills or a candidate's ability to showcase deep expertise in the field through what they have already achieved.

However, the more people I meet and the more data points I have correlating talent in their interviews and eventual performance, I realise what really makes an employee standout and for their high performance to be sustainable is not their outward ability to make an impression and connection, but the qualities that are inward and innate—which are often too difficult to observe. I have seen leaders aggressively architect their rise in the hierarchy by jumping ship and delivering impressive storyboards of their past successes, but then failing to translate to actual success in their new organisations. This is typically exemplified by disengaged teams and stakeholders, and often coincides with feedback from the market that often comes in too late.

I have also observed the quiet talent that changes organisations with the motivation to learn and grow often excel through every single transition. One of the most well-rounded HR leaders I have had the privilege to work with on my team was initially unsuccessful in getting hired onto my team due to zero experience in the industry. The role we were hiring for would not have set her up for success. She was understandably disappointed, but she followed up with a clear and succinct note on how she saw the role, the team, the leader, and the organisation as an opportunity for growth. It contained a clear outline of what that growth plan could look like for her and how she planned to achieve those learnings, even though she had never worked for a hyper-growth technology company. Her ability to articulate her plans from a growth mindset really made an impression, and she was hired a few months later when an appropriate role opened up. At the time of this writing, this HR leader continues to excel and grow in completely different industries because of her growth mindset.

"What do you look for in a candidate during the interview?"

The answer is a lot more straightforward these days: *a strong growth mindset.*

This answer is often met with scepticism or confusion. What is a growth mindset? What does it look like? And is it a capability that can be built and developed?

Let us continue to explore how it is possible to cultivate a growth mindset.

A growth mindset is cultivated by activating curiosity and practising grit.

Growth mindset = curiosity × grit

* * *

In the following chapters, we will dive deeper into a constructive approach to cultivating a growth mindset through activating curiosity and practising grit. The proposed notion here is that a growth mindset is a muscle that can be trained and practised to maintain our growth mindset elasticity. More importantly, a growth mindset can only be meaningful and productive when it is applied within a context. In other words, simply having a growth mindset does not equate to meaningful and productive outcomes.

I propose nurturing a growth mindset as a way of being and a way to approach problem-solving. A growth mindset can be elevated and harnessed with practical strategies. In Part II, I will offer strategies for developing a growth mindset centred around activating curiosity and practising grit. I will also call out the need to foster self-reflection habits as the starting point before we dive into further strategies.

Before proposing the strategies for developing a growth mindset, it is important to obtain a deeper understanding of the concept from Carol Dweck. Dweck pioneered the concept of a growth mindset through her early childhood research. Many years later after her first publication on the topic, Dweck called out that people often confuse a growth mindset with being open-minded or flexible, which are qualities they already possess. She termed this as a "false growth mindset." In reality, we are all a mixture of fixed and growth mindsets, and that mixture continues to evolve with our life experiences.

A "pure" growth mindset does not exist, and it is not what we should strive for. Therefore, the notion of "cultivating" a growth mindset is not an attempt to eliminate the fixed mindset, but to take an intentional approach to optimising the growth mindset that we have and utilising it in our work as HR leaders.

In summary, this part of the book will propose several strategies for cultivating a growth mindset.

Three proposed strategies activate curiosity through:

1. Cultivating a learning habit
2. Slowing down and not jumping into the first solution
3. Reliving the joy of experimenting

Four proposed strategies practise grit through:

1. Pursuing your passion—with focus
2. Practising deep learning
3. Sharing your failures and learning from criticisms
4. Surrounding yourself with gritty people

I also provide some space for reflection by proposing reflective inquiry activities under each of the strategies framed by research around growth mindset, curiosity, and grit.

This part of the book will offer some contextual commentaries on how each component may surface in the HR context, but essentially, the strategies can be understood and applied in different contexts that are most relevant for you.

CHAPTER 3

Foster Self-Reflection Habits as the Starting Point for a Growth Mindset

Early in my career, I used to feel the need to have all the answers, but it turns out that a continuous outward search for answers blocks my ability to self-reflect. I was tired of seeking answers rather than asking meaningful questions—to others and to myself. I felt like I had reached a self-imposed block in my career, despite the fact that I had always been hailed as having "high potential" or being a "high performer."

It was not until I hit that ultimate mental block that I knew I had to do something drastically different to jumpstart my learning again. After exploring many academic options, I took a leap of faith forward.

I quit my comfortable lead role as a regional HR business partner in a well-regarded financial technology company and moved to Jakarta, Indonesia. I knew no one—no friends, no family. The only thing that was pushing me forward was knowing I could be in the heart of Southeast Asia, learning what working on the ground looks like for an emerging Asian startup. I took on an HR leadership role that had a strong focus on business transformation through people.

My growth mindset was unleashed.

* * *

A growth mindset is not a novel concept. It has been widely researched in the context of early childhood psychology and education, and was later applied in more adult settings. In her 2006 book *Mindset: The New Psychology for Success*, Dweck suggests there are two types of mindsets: a growth mindset and a fixed mindset. Her research findings suggest that individuals can be placed on a continuum according to their implicit views on where ability comes from. Individuals with a fixed mindset believe that success is based on an innate ability and cannot be changed, while individuals with a growth mindset believe that success is based on hard work, learning, and training, which can be developed.

The sense of helplessness observed within the fixed mindset suggests that such individuals are more likely to be passive when dealing with challenges and may revert back to known answers, such as best practices, to resolve issues. On the other hand, the active and reflective components of the growth mindset point to the ability to explore new practices by taking a deeper and more curious approach to understanding the problem at hand.

By extension, the belief that a growth mindset can be developed suggests it is possible to derive ways to learn and experiment to foster that mindset. It is not an intangible quality that can never be captured.

One of the key components involved in fostering a growth mindset is the role of praise or external validation. Research by Dweck in 2010 showed that children who had been praised for their intellect were more likely to choose easier puzzles when given a choice. Children who had been praised for their effort were more likely to persist in the harder task and request another challenging puzzle. In the adult learning and HR leader context, the notion of "praise" may be translated to performance reviews, promotions, or the ability to respond to requests from the CEO that mirror best practices requests.

Fixed mindsets do not appreciate failure because failure is seen as a negative statement about their innate abilities, which they cannot change. On the other hand, those with growth mindsets approach failure as an opportunity to learn and improve. The way we process external and internal validations will likely impact how we continue to foster our growth mindset.

I am not equating a fixed mindset to an inability to be successful in a career. It is very plausible that one can become competent and functionally fluent in a capability with a fixed mindset through passive knowledge acquisition. Think of a very competent accountant who has passed all the exams and tests, and is very likely able to perform the role really well and function on a daily basis as long as fixed solutions to problems are expected.

However, not every competent accountant can become a future

CFO, even when the financial issues that CFOs must address can be answered by the textbook and best practices. There could be many differentiating factors, ranging from ambitions to interests. However, assuming the ambitions are equal, the way that one activates and channels their curiosity would be the make-or-break quality for an individual hoping to learn deeply about finance, as well as the numerous variables within the practice of finance, such as mergers and acquisitions or international expansion, to advance their career as the CFO. This is not to oversimplify career progression and advancement, but this makes the case for one's ability to become a deep expert through curiosity and grit, which in turn, cultivates their growth mindset.

Research on brain plasticity also suggests that connectivity between neurons can change with experience. This is to say that, with practice, it is possible to foster a growth mindset by the actions we take. A growth mindset should be understood as a tendency to be fluid rather than absolute. However, it is not all or nothing; you can have a strong growth mindset towards one thing and a more fixed mindset towards another.

Take myself as an example. My growth mindset can be exemplified by tackling various academic pursuits while working full time, but I would much prefer to ask my husband for directions to a new location than to look at a map or pretend that I am even remotely interested in it. On most day, I am excited about doing challenging work and juggle multiple projects at once. On some days, I find my pursuit of multiple projects tiring and just want to have a day of doing absolutely nothing. Having a growth mindset does not mean you are on this endless pursuit of learning and growth. That would be unproductive and tiring.

Not forgetting that your brain is a muscle and all the top athletes will tell you that a good rest goes a long way in building up muscle and energy sustainably.

It is likely that you have a default mindset tendency that is also observable to others. I encourage you to consider the reality of your growth mindset by talking to those who work closely with you and asking them to provide input on your growth mindset tendencies.

Does a growth mindset translate to career success?

It depends on how you define career success, but it is also impacted by on how your operating environment appreciates and rewards a growth mindset.

"Tell me what Google or Netflix does" are some of the most uttered words from the mouths of senior executives in technology industries, and it signals an operating environment that may not appreciate a growth mindset. This environment is likely not going to set the growth-minded HR leader up for career success. The question often sends the HR teams into a frenzy trying to find the answers, even though it is almost impossible without being fully immersed in the context of Google. There is an underlying assumption that because it worked for Google, it will work for all—and lead any company to be just as successful as Google is.

What we often do not do but should do is pause and ask,

Under what context and set of conditions did this HR practice work for Google?

WHAT DOES A GROWTH MINDSET MEAN TO YOU?

To begin cultivating a growth mindset, there is the fundamental requirement to foster self-reflection.

Part of the motivation to develop a growth mindset is to understand the natural mindset tendencies of yourself and others. In some cases, these tendencies may be cultural (i.e., early education experiences in Asia may foster a fixed mindset by focusing solely on exam results) or career-dependent (i.e., working in mostly mature companies may lead you to become more structured in policy guidance when it comes to managing people challenges). Identifying these tendencies can really help us better understand our motivations and how to adapt our own learning strategies and solution tendencies accordingly.

This realisation hit me the hardest once I started working in Indonesia, a completely different environment that was out of my comfort zone. I had previously studied and practised HR in mostly developed countries. I had enjoyed the progressive HR transformation bubble in New Zealand, Norway, the United Kingdom, and Singapore, where we had the luxury of a considerably high talent density and financial resources to improve HR.

I had a skewed HR exposure, and I needed to get out. I felt a sense of superficiality in my HR practices, and I need to go deeper in understanding how HR can transform in fundamentally different contexts. I was excelling in my job at the outset, but it felt flat. It felt one-dimensional.

I felt like a great swimmer who did not know how to dive or swim outside the comfort of a heated lap pool.

Self-reflection in the context of a growth mindset involves diving deeper into your success and unpacking the more sustainable learning that is required to maintain and deepen your current success. This type of self-reflection is tough because it is almost counterproductive and counterintuitive. It asks you to consider what is not working, even though you may be at the peak of your success. It requires you to take a big step back, explore the future, and humbly anticipate pitfalls.

I realised that I needed to get into emerging markets and learn from the ground up how to operate in an environment where there are no heated lap pools—only unpredictable and foreign waves. I quit the secure role I was performing in Singapore and moved to Jakarta, Indonesia. I joined a growing primary healthcare company focusing on the development of pharmacy practices in the second-tier cities of Indonesia. That meant moving to a place where I had no personal or professional network—and where I did not speak the local language. I had no friends, no family, and no words of Bahasa. The real sharp learning curve truly began.

Focusing on self-reflection in the context of a growth mindset allows you to pinpoint and explore your growth mindset blockers and blind spots. Growth mindset blind spots articulate your barrier to deep learning. It is important to discover such barriers, as they ultimately limit your ability to cultivate curiosity and are the roadblock to unleashing your growth mindset.

My growth mindset blind spot is that, at times, I am overly eager to learn new things but unable to fully engage in the in-depth learning that is required to excel. I often get excited about the idea of learning something, but I may not be able to invest the time or energy to truly accomplish it. I have picked up and given up a number of learning pursuits, including interior design, baking, and acrylic painting. At the start, I was committed to each, but that commitment diminished over time as I realised that the time commitment required to truly excel was almost impossible given the other commitments in my life.

To a large extent, my growth mindset blind spot and roadblock is my own curiosity and perfectionism. When I realise that I do not have the capacity to fully excel in something and be "perfect" at it, I would rather stop than learn superficially. We can debate whether that is a helpful way to think or not, but the most important part of this strategy is to first be aware of the curiosity blind spot. It serves as a guidepost for how you might spend your energy learning in the future.

In my learning journey, I have made peace with the fact that I am best when I focus on a few things and excel at them. I still maintain interest in many things, which I can simply read or listen to podcasts about or watch documentaries on to satisfy my curiosities.

Some reflective inquiry practice questions that could be useful to identify your growth mindset blind spots are:

- *What was my last attempt to learn something that failed? What have I learnt from that?*
- *What was my last attempt to learn something that succeeded? What have I learnt from that?*

- *How do I feel when I receive negative feedback about my work?*
- *What do I do when I receive negative feedback about my work?*
- *How do I keep going when I am stuck on a problem?*
- *In what environment do I learn the best?*

In the context of HR, fostering self-reflection allows you to not rely on best practices when dealing with business challenges. As an HR leader, you are likely surrounded by HR issues of different magnitudes daily. Often, repetitive or relatively small issues may be met with tried-and-tested solutions rather than investing the energy and effort on seeking out other solutions. It is often assumed that a deep dive into issues is better suited for organisational issues, such as low engagement scores or high turnovers.

For example, when a leader complains about the performance of their direct report, a fixed mindset approach may revert to activating performance improvement plans, while a growth mindset approach may seek to understand the broader context that may influence employee performance, such as larger economic viability, team dynamics, or even an employee's personal issues. Understanding the deeper dynamic that may influence the problem—regardless of if it is big or small—as well as the symptoms that present on the surface will promote the opportunity to solve root issues.

REFLECTIVE INQUIRY PRACTICES

- *What is your growth mindset blind spot?*

- *How has the blind spot shown up in your life?*

- *How has the blind spot shown up in your career as an HR leader?*

A Growth Mindset Is Cultivated by Two Cornerstone Capabilities— Curiosity and Grit

It feels like I have been on a crusade for growth mindsets in organisations and HR settings for the better part of the last decade in my career. Although people nod with sparkles in their eyes after my impassioned speech, I often receive feedback that "growth mindset" seems more like a new-age buzzword than a practical framework to grasp and practise. Although various recommendations and tools have been introduced in early childhood education and some adult reflections, it remains a challenging concept to grasp, especially in a professional setting.

This chapter seeks to bring two cornerstone capabilities—curiosity and grit—to the forefront as we think about cultivating a growth mindset in ways that are not just conceptual but practical.

FROM COMPETENCY FRAMEWORKS TO CORNERSTONE CAPABILITIES

As HR leaders, we are used to working with competency frameworks that attempt to capture the capabilities necessary to be successful within an organisation. Most organisations have between six and ten defined capabilities, and some have many more. There are also competency frameworks that are not organisation-wide but rather organised by functions and roles. These could easily be calibrated to hundreds of competencies deemed important for the success of employees. The concept of a competency framework screams "best practice."

According to the Chartered Institute of Personnel and Development (CIPD)—a well-established professional association for human resource management professionals with roots in the United Kingdom—the term "competency" focuses on personal attributes or inputs, which are technical and behavioural attributes that enable teams to perform effectively at work. Therefore, a "competency framework" is a structure that sets out and defines each individual competency (such as problem-solving or people management) required by individuals working in an organisation or part of that organisation.

By definition, competency frameworks stem from the best practice tradition of thinking about capabilities, growth, and performance. The concept emerged during the early 1980s as a response to bringing structure and directional guides to organisational development to drive higher performance levels. Competency frameworks were first designed with behavioural elements as the key components. This was in response to a need to foster the softer skills involved in effective performance alongside technical competencies. More and more, competency frameworks have since become broader in scope to include both soft and technical skillsets.

More captivating names have been used to describe competency frameworks, such as growth frameworks and job architecture, which linked competency frameworks to job levelling and titles within their respective organisations. During subsequent decades, competency frameworks have become an increasingly accepted part of HR practices. The competency framework is embedded in many other HR practices, such as recruitment and selection, where competency-based interviews remain popular.

CIPD remains a strong advocate for competency frameworks, believing that they can be useful to support talent strategies and guide practices in areas such as recruitment, talent development, and performance management. CIPD does note, however, that for any competency framework to be successful in supporting talent-based decision-making, it must accurately reflect the needs of both the organisation and the specific roles in question in terms of skills, experience, and behaviours, as well as reflecting the organisation's ethos and values.

The competency framework's relevance to this discussion is twofold. First, the competency framework is the pinnacle of best practices in HR. It is the go-to for HR leaders when they are thinking about redesigning HR practices in their organisations. More and more, we adopt an even more complex approach to the competency framework, articulating it by roles, seniority/job levels, and functions within an organisation, which could easily lead to more than hundreds of competency frameworks that duplicate one another or, in some cases, are non-complementary.

As the world and organisations we operate in become even more complex, the people solutions we offer as HR leaders may need to be simpler and perhaps more elegant in their communication and execution. It may be time for us to move away from competency frameworks altogether. We must instead think of the core capabilities that act as the cornerstones to capability development. Cornerstone capabilities are intended to be focused with agility in application across roles and hierarchy within organisations.

In thinking about cultivating a growth mindset within the frame of identifying competencies, we look to the two cornerstone capabilities for a growth mindset: *curiosity* and *grit*.

The idea of a cornerstone capability is that it is the foundation upon which all other capabilities are built. In essence, without curiosity and grit, all the required common competencies, such as stakeholder management or effective communication, become superficial in nature. Curiosity allows for individuals to learn deeply and translate knowledge agilely, and grit allows for the continuous improvement and consistent engagement needed to thrive and create a substantial impact through other identified capabilities.

CURIOSITY AS A CORNERSTONE
CAPABILITY AND A STATE OF MIND

Curiosity is not an action but a state of mind. By acknowledging and introducing curiosity as a capability, we must assume that curiosity is something that one can learn and continue to excel in. Curiosity allows our brains to be in a state of openness that motivates us to learn and retain new information. As Dr. Matthias Gruber, a researcher at the University of California-Davis, put it nicely, "Curiosity may put the brain in a state that allows it to learn and retain any kind of information, like a vortex that sucks in what you are motivated to learn and also everything around it."

CURIOSITY STARTS WITH INTELLECTUAL EMPATHY

The concept of intellectual empathy brings forth a multidimensional framework to think about curiosity and HR practices. Intellectual empathy is generally referred to as the ability for someone to actively put themself in someone else's shoes in terms of how they think and feel to support insightful decision-making. The word "intellectual" differentiates the more passive understanding of "empathy" by adding the active pursuit of critical thinking to the baseline of empathy. Without activating curiosity, it would be impossible for us to truly engage in intellectual empathy that could make sustainable and meaningful differences. Intellectual empathy allows us to shift from "I can feel your pain" to "I seek to understand your pain through questioning my own current understanding and taking active actions to ensure that it is reflected in the solutions and decision-making." This activation is important for HR leaders, as we are tasked with recommending people and organisational solutions that will inevitably impact another person's life deeply.

Intellectual empathy was introduced by Maureen Linker, a philosophy professor at the University of Michigan-Dearborn. She developed the concept of intellectual empathy after more than a decade of teaching critical thinking in metropolitan Detroit. Linker uses the concept to develop practical approaches and strategies for educators, activists, business managers, and community leaders in pursuit of meaningful dialogues about social differences. Linker advocates for the skills that are required to develop intellectual empathy in the same way that I now advocate for curiosity and grit as the cornerstone capabilities to develop a growth mindset.

The five skills necessary for intellectual empathy include:

- Understanding the invisibility of privilege
- Knowing that social identity is intersectional
- Using the model of cooperative reasoning
- Applying the principles of conditional trust
- Recognising our mutual vulnerability

The reason I introduce the concept of intellectual empathy in the context of being a growth-minded HR leader is to remind all of us that the impact of our work goes beyond just individuals, teams, or even a company. It impacts the communities in which we operate.

Organisations, at scale, often reflect the social construction of the society we operate in. Our work is intertwined with the business and, in turn, impacts the community. We are not discussing intellectual empathy in the way of social responsibility, but in the way of being a building block of the communities in which we operate. The five skills outlined above are helpful frameworks in the context of HR as we think through the impact of our HR practices and how they relate to social construction and social justice.

HR policies that channel intellectual empathy could be represented by equal maternity and paternity leaves or supporting "return to work" for employees that had an extended break from work due to personal reasons. Intellectual empathy does not require us to choose a side, but it does require us to be curious in pursuing a deeper understanding of different views and experiences and in developing appropriate and impactful people solutions that reflect such an understanding.

Intellectual empathy in action for HR leaders empowers us to ask the right questions activated by curiosity. Questions channelling intellectual empathy could look like:

- *How does our performance review consider the invisibility of privilege across global offices?*
- *How does our company culture recognise intersectional social identity?*
- *How do our leaders model cooperative reasoning?*
- *And how do conditional trust and mutual vulnerability manifest in our organisation?*

CURIOSITY AT WORK: FROM AN
EMPLOYEE'S PERSPECTIVE

As we dive deeper into curiosity in the contexts of growth-minded HR and within the organisational contexts, we may soon realise something obvious. New technology has granted us unlimited access to information, and knowledge acquisition is just a button away for employees. As much as we may talk about the skills needed for the future and why they might be in short supply, the organisations of today actually do not have a skills problem.

We have a curiosity problem.

Employees attend learning and development programs in the workplace for several reasons: out of necessity, out of desire for career advancement, and out of curiosity. Of these, curiosity has perhaps the greatest value and is a higher predictor of enhanced performance.

Like all complex yet beautifully simple concepts, there is no one clear definition of curiosity. The *Cambridge Dictionary* defines it as an eager wish to learn about something. Taking a more philosophical and psychological view, William James, the first educator to offer a psychology course in the United States, suggested that curiosity can be understood as the desire and impulse to understand what you do not and a drive for better cognition.

Curiosity drives individuals to improve themselves, not just in our professional lives but also in our personal lives. A potential product of curiosity is a cross-pollination of ideas between our personal and professional lives. Therefore, when we, as HR leaders, discuss a growth mindset in action, we assume an all-around growth mindset shift, which will positively impact an individual professionally and personally.

In his book *Originals,* Adam Grant quotes a Michigan State University study that found that Nobel Prize winners were significantly more likely to be involved in the arts than less accomplished scientists. The study compared every Nobel Prize–winning scientist from 1901 to 2005 and found that engagement in the arts, like music, fine art, writing, and performing, increased their odds of winning the Nobel Prize up to twenty-two times. Another representative study of thousands of Americans showed similar results for entrepreneurs and inventors. This suggests that pursuing personal interests outside of work, such as in the arts, not only reflects one's curiosity and aptitude but can also serve as a powerful source of creative insight at work.

Curiosity in the workplace can manifest in two ways: (1) through the active provision of learning sources, from books to stretch assignments, and (2) through the organisational culture that embraces the process and outcomes of curiosity. The first is perhaps much easier to fulfil, while the second requires us to reflect and build intentionally.

What does a curious learning organisational culture look like?

In a curious learning culture, managers or leaders provide their employees with the opportunity to experiment and fail without fear of judgement—or a negative performance review. A curious learning culture is therefore built on the psychological safety to fail and learn. A curious learning culture is modelled by leaders who demonstrate transparency and open communication, particularly around uncomfortable topics, and who build trust with their teams and encourage feedback from a place of improvement and moving forward together as a team. A curious learning culture is also activated by leaders asking thoughtful questions when teams bring forth new ideas and suggestions.

We can nurture a curious learning culture by building learning experiences and journeys that are curiosity-driven. This entails building a community of knowledge and experience sharing, as well as promoting self-directed learning accountabilities. As we attempt to build a community of curious learners, we must acknowledge the importance of both the self and the community within this transformation.

For HR leaders, understanding and activating curiosity at work is the guiding principle in what we do and how we design learning journeys. It is worth drawing our attention to why activating or cultivating adult curiosity is much more challenging than doing so in children. Christy Geiger, a *Forbes* contributing coach and writer, shared the same sentiments when she pointed out what she calls "curiosity shutdowns" in adults. Geiger suggests that curiosity is in shutdown mode when we think we know all the answers and are considered experts. Such a mindset shift means that instead of fostering a culture of curiosity, we instead look to foster competition to become experts, which is, of course, amplified by our egos.

When we think we know everything, is our learning done?

∗ ∗ ∗

GRIT AS A CORNERSTONE CAPABILITY
AMPLIFIES CURIOSITY

"What is the one defining factor for talent in an organisation?"

Throughout my years of observing talent within my work as a talent developer, this is another one of the most common questions I hear.

My answer remains consistent: "Someone with a growth mindset."

It is also my consistent response when my own team member asks for the one expectation I have of them or when I am quizzed on what I think is the key to a team's success.

This expectation is a two-way street. It calls for individuals to take accountability for their own learning and how they show up in challenging situations. It also calls for leaders to appreciate and cultivate an environment that fosters a growth mindset in their own teams, which often means building a safe space to experiment and grow through mistakes.

"How do we develop a growth mindset?" is often the follow-up question.

As alluded to earlier, a growth mindset results from the cultivation of two cornerstone capabilities: curiosity and grit. It is an active and continuous process and not an outcome. We touched on curiosity earlier, so now let us take a deeper look at grit.

Grit is important within the equation of the growth mindset because, without grit, curiosity may become a directionless passion and infatuation with all things that pique your interest. Without curiosity, grit may manifest as the stubbornness to pursue a path superficially and without considering other options.

Angela Duckworth puts it nicely in her 2019 book, Grit: The Power of Passion and Perseverance. She writes that grit has two components: passion and perseverance. Passion is about pursuing something with intense consistency over time. It is not just a one-off. Grit amplifies curiosity by providing a consistent guiding star for your energy, which leads you on a path towards greater outcomes.

Duckworth frames the concept of grit and success succinctly when she suggests that achieving extraordinary success is not about being a genius or the smartest in the room, but about being the grittiest. Duckworth reminds us that many of our perceptions of success are framed and developed through the lens of cultural expectations, such as the Asian family's traditional view of success being linked to working as a doctor or a lawyer.

Our upbringing becomes the catalyst for our own interpretation of success. I grew up in Taiwan in a rather high-pressure "tiger mum" environment. With all good intentions, my mother continues to compare me with my brother and with the "smart neighbour" upstairs. In her eyes, those were the benchmarks of my success. I resonate with Duckworth's notions of upbringing and expectations from parents—and the inevitable attempt to make our parents proud through the shallow recognition of our academic achievement.

I have yet to receive a genius award, unlike Duckworth, but the reflection on her own Asian upbringing still resonates. Though as a child I was constantly reminded that I was not the smartest (or prettiest—or even remotely okay-looking) girl in the class, I ended up with a PhD and a rewarding career in HR. More than anything, I am the product of grit and curiosity. My grit is exemplified by my endless endeavours to learn and share my learning with the teams I lead and the wider community. I always tell aspiring PhD candidates that I have a PhD not because I am smart but because I am curious and persistent. My curiosity drove me to want to dive deep into the phenomenon of interest—my PhD thesis was on psychological implications of knowledge management in times of organisational changes, framed by the macro environment of an ageing workforce—and understand it from many angles through intense research of individuals, organisations, and teams in various locations. My curiosity means that I want to be able to develop insights about a topic and share those insights with a community of learners. These are the attributes that led me to a doctorate degree. Getting a doctorate was never the starting point. Curiosity was.

I would like to end this chapter with the reminder that grit amplifies curiosity. Curiosity fuels the start of a pursuit, and grit ensures it gets done.

Coming back to why a growth mindset matters as an HR leader and why I have relentlessly pursued a growth mindset myself, I reflect back on the evolution of HR covered earlier in this book. HR is and has been at a crossroads for decades. I find that many of us are struggling, and some, strutting at the crossroads, are unwilling to leap into the brave new world of HR. In this new world, we are not gatekeepers, parental figures, or police. We are coaches and equally respected strategic partners in our organisations' success. We may demand change and recognition without fully articulating or acting on the changes required from within.

I believe in sustainable change through collective change. We cannot achieve such collective change without activating change at the individual level. Therefore, in the next chapters, we will look more closely at practical, strategic steps to activate curiosity and practise grit as HR leaders.

CHAPTER 5

Strategies to Activate Curiosity

By this point in the book, we have made a case for the importance of activating curiosity as part of cultivating a growth
mindset as an HR leader.

On the surface level, this chapter can easily be read as a general
strategy for cultivating a growth mindset as adults. However,
the key element that differentiates the operating environment
for HR leaders is the people-related problem-solving that our
profession centres on. Compared to the problem-solving that
may be linked to more logical approaches and outcomes, such
as mathematical puzzles or structural landscape design, the
problems that HR leaders encounter and are required to solve
on a daily basis are often emotionally charged. In other words,
HR issues only emerge as such because they evoke emotions—
and, more often than not, negative ones.

As shared earlier, a growth mindset does not lead to an outcome without being framed in the context one operates in. We will highlight the strategies using HR-specific examples because it is not only important to think about a growth mindset in the context of learning, but also in problem-solving in relation to human emotions and the psyche. Recognising the innate nature of human emotions in association with the problems that HR leaders are trying to solve allows for a growth-minded HR practice to respond in a way that connects with those emotions. I want to stress the emotional elements of HR problem-solving before we dive into the strategies outlined below because they inform the foundation for your technical know-how in HR. Before you start solving the problem, explore and understand the emotions involved. Acknowledge the emotions first and build on your intellectual empathy.

Cultivating a growth mindset is not dissimilar to running a marathon. Think of it this way: if your desired outcome is to complete a marathon, having adequate strategies to train your stamina and health will help you prepare for that, but those strategies will not necessarily determine the marathon route you will eventually take. Running a marathon is an appropriate analogy because cultivating and practising a growth mindset is a marathon. It requires the same motivation, stamina, and passion to sustain it.

As we continue to think about activating curiosity, I challenge you to think about it circularly and holistically. Let us consider how we activate curiosity in ourselves as well as how to activate curiosity in others as leaders.

Let us start with a deeper exploration of ourselves.

Curiosity in practice comes down to three ways of thinking:

1. Admitting that you do not know everything
2. Holding the belief that there is never just one way to solve a problem
3. Having the desire to explore different ways to solve a problem

This baseline curiosity mindset allows you to dive deep into the strategies below and engage with the proposed actions in a more meaningful way.

Strategies to activate curiosity:

1. Cultivate a learning habit—read, read, and read some more.
2. Slow down. Do not jump into the first solution. Ask questions instead.
3. Relive the joy of experimenting.

* * *

STRATEGY 1: CULTIVATING A LEARNING HABIT

We learn differently. Some of us like reading books, some of us like podcasts, and some of us like discussion forums. Whatever your preferred medium, the act of regular learning is a game changer. According to researchers at Duke University, habits account for about 40 per cent of our behaviours on any given day, many of which are small and done on autopilot. Think of that morning coffee or that book you bring on your commute.

James Clear, in his book *Atomic Habits*, speaks of practical strategies for building new habits. Clear describes starting with incredibly small habits. This could be reading one LinkedIn article of interest while you drink your morning coffee or three pages of a book before bed. Make it small and easy—so easy that your perceived effort does not become the roadblock to your learning habit. Clear also suggests that once you begin a small habit, you can increase it in many ways, like expanding from reading one article with your morning coffee to two.

My small learning habit is to devote ten minutes at the start of my workday to reading something interesting or reflecting on something. Just ten minutes.

Clear also suggests a great strategy of breaking habits into smaller chunks. For example, as you build from reading two articles to five articles a day, break it into three different time periods: morning, lunch, and before bed, perhaps. Importantly, as Clear points out, building habits is not a sprint, and you should stick to a pace you can sustain. It is better to sustain the energy and interest to read one article a day over six months than to aim to read three articles a day and give up after one month due to the velocity of the commitment.

Cultivating learning habits is important in the context of a growth mindset. The act of learning reminds us that we do not have the answers to everything and that there are various perspectives on things.

REFLECTIVE INQUIRY PRACTICES

- *What are you learning at the moment? Or what would you like to be learning?*

- *What was the last learning medium that you enjoyed (or currently enjoy)?*

- *What does your learning habit look like at present?*

- *How much time can you reasonably commit to learning a week?*

- *If there is one thing you want to change with your learning habit, what does it look like?*

STRATEGY 2: SLOW DOWN. DO NOT JUMP INTO THE FIRST SOLUTION. ASK QUESTIONS INSTEAD.

The best practice mindset prescribes solutions and outcomes. That is why it is so comfortable. We have precedence we can refer to and map towards, and we have outcomes we can anticipate and turn to should situations fail to turn out as intended. For decades, companies valued best practices masked in the brand of innovation. We see companies investing in management consultants precisely because they bring best practices and implementation experiences to the table.

A practical approach to activating curiosity is to ask inquisitive questions of yourself and others. By asking questions, we activate two impactful aspects of curiosity: (1) a coaching mindset and (2) active listening.

A coaching mindset reminds us that our role is to provoke insight by inviting others to think deeper and reflect within themselves rather than thinking for them by providing them the answers. This is challenging because our brains, especially as leaders, are wired to answer questions, solve problems, and fix issues. By asking questions, we open a world of opportunities that allows us to learn new insights in return, and those insights become the foundation for formulating growth practices.

What insightful questions have you asked yourself or those around you today?

Good, impactful questions are often open-ended and encourage engaging, free-flowing answers. Open-ended questions usually lead to expansive discussions that address not only the topic but also tangential issues surrounding the topic. This is not to say that closed-ended questions have no place in activating curiosity or in powering a coaching mindset. In fact, it is often helpful to use yes or no questions to establish or confirm facts that will ultimately contribute to the broader approach of problem-solving.

The value of your solution is in the eye of the beholder.

Active listening is an important element of activating curiosity because it is the bridge between asking questions and providing insightful recommendations—recommendations that are not based on prescribed answers. The Centre for Creative Leadership, a leading leadership development consulting practice, breaks down active listening into six components: *pay attention, withhold judgement, reflect, clarify, summarise, and share.* Active listening is first about understanding another person and then about being understood.

Paying attention sets a safe space for the speaker to have an opportunity to think and speak. Allow wait time before responding. Be focused on the moment, make eye contact, and operate from a place of respect as the listener.

Withholding judgement allows us to be open to new ideas, perspectives, and possibilities. Listening is not about looking for information to confirm the bias you may have towards the outcome.

Reflecting helps prevent you from assuming that you understand everything you hear, including information and emotions. Periodically paraphrasing key points to confirm understanding helps to ensure you and the speakers are on the same page.

Clarifying using open-ended and probing questions is an important active listening tool that encourages everyone in the conversation to self-reflect and problem-solve together. There is no one right answer.

Summarising may feel simple, but it is critical because it confirms and solidifies your grasp of the other person's point of view. It also helps both parties to be clear on mutual responsibilities and follow-up.

Share your views when appropriate, and ask for permission before sharing. Asking for permission is a powerful way to allow your speaker to shift their mindset from speaking to listening.

REFLECTIVE INQUIRY PRACTICES

- *Pay attention the next time someone comes to you with a problem. What mindset do you gravitate towards?*
  - *What is usually your first sentence after someone has shared a problem with you?*

- *Reflect on how well you actively listen by taking a conscious review of these six components: pay attention, withhold judgement, reflect, clarify, summarise, and share.*
  - *What are the conditions that allow you to be deeper in your active listening?*

STRATEGY 3: RELIVE THE JOY OF EXPERIMENTING

There is no set path or single way to reach our goals and the outcomes we strive for as HR leaders. We face new situations and challenges every day—and we cannot always anticipate them.

When we detach from the mindset of best practices and instead embrace curiosity and grit to drive innovative ideas, then much of what we attempt will be experimental. Those experiments will not all be perfect. The important thing to remember is to keep refining your experiments until they yield the outcome intended. Bear in mind that what is right for your organisation at one moment in time may change in a year or two (or maybe even in six months).

The trick is to keep experimenting, gathering data, analysing, and then refining your approach—again and again.

There is no end to your experiments, just as there are no perfect answers to find.

The key to activating curiosity may not necessarily be the act of experimenting but the ability to reclaim the joy of it. I have a two-year-old toddler at the time of this writing, and I often marvel at the pure joy in his eyes when he tries new things, whether it is loosening the cap of a water bottle or putting his green dinosaur puzzle together. He tries each new approach with energy and determination. Even after a number of unsuccessful attempts, he never loses his determination or joy during the process.

The joy of experimenting fuels the activation of curiosity.

That joy comes from focusing on thought processes and solutions. Using thought processes to form testable hypotheses will allow us to experiment and confirm the hypothesis that may lead to a proposed solution. That thought process may look as simple as understanding external trends and collecting internal data to analyse how the data resonates with those trends.

This does not mean that the solution will be perfect right away. And that is fine. It is okay if it takes you a number of tries before you settle on the most appropriate solution at that moment for your organisation. Giving yourself and your teams permission to experiment instead of turning to best practices will ultimately benefit everyone involved.

We, as HR leaders, must be willing to step outside of the comfort of best practices to focus on the problem we are really trying to solve.

We do not assume that all businesses have a one-size-fits-all strategy, so why should we do just that with HR practices? The one-size-fits-all approach to HR leads to mediocre results. Many business leaders have made innovation a top priority for their companies—it is how they ensure their companies remain competitive in a quickly changing world. We hear about product and technology innovation. We hear about innovation in the supply chain. We hear about innovation in marketing and promotions. But we do not hear about innovation in HR practices nearly as often as we should. Why is that?

Every organisation and the challenges its employees face are framed by their own unique circumstances. Channelling and taking action by deeply engaging in understanding the unique organisational setting requires HR leaders to adopt agile thinking.

The concept of agility in business was first made popular alongside IT development, which implemented multiple agile methodologies, such as systematic customer resolution unravelling meetings (better known as SCRUM) and disciplined agile delivery management (DADM). A positive correlation between agility and higher human performance was discovered by one of the leading global management consulting firms, McKinsey. McKinsey's research proved that the more someone can employ agile thinking, the higher their performance. When we think of agility, we usually apply this to a business and its ability to rapidly respond to market changes by altering its strategies. It is a term that has gained prominence in recent years as market disruptions have increased in number and speed.

Agility, or agile thinking, has equal application and power when applied to HR practices. I would go so far as to say that agile thinking is a *requirement* for HR leaders. The markets we operate in move extremely fast, with changes coming at us from all directions. This rapidly shifting environment requires HR leaders to think quickly—and differently. Agile thinking is the ability to think differently about a challenge without frustration or confusion and to develop an innovative solution for it. It is the ability to provide a solution that has never been heard of or done before.

Agility is not the same as a growth mindset, but it does complement it. Agility is a skill that allows one to continue adapting to change. It may be coupled with learning from failure and continuing to find joy in experiments.

REFLECTIVE INQUIRY PRACTICES

- *How do you speak about best practices?*
  - *How do you feel when someone speaks about best practice solutions?*

- *On a scale of one to ten (ten being the highest), how much do you enjoy experiments?*
  - *Can you share examples that elaborate on the score you shared?*

- *What does "experimenting" look like and mean for you?*
  - *What does "experimenting" look like and mean for your teams and/or organisation?*
  - *Is there a gap in perception?*

- *How often do you experiment and what drives the frequency?*

Curiosity activation is not accidental, nor is it a force of nature that cannot be nurtured.

If you continuously practise activating your curiosity through the strategies outlined above and embrace the reflective nature of curiosity, you will become more fluent in your own curiosity mindset and practices.

With the mindset shift to admitting that you do not know everything and holding the belief that there is never just one way to solve a problem, you create a place where different ways to solve a problem can be explored.

This baseline curious mindset allows you to dive deep into the curiosity activation strategies to cultivate a meaningful and sustainable learning habit, be intentional with problem-solving powered by questions, and relive the joy of experimentation by embracing the vulnerability of not knowing.

This activated curiosity will now be your anchor to practise grit.

Chapter 6

Strategies to Practise Grit

What is grit?

In her book *Grit,* Duckworth defines grit as "our passion and perseverance for long-term goals." Meaningfully, Duckworth notes that grit does not mean talent. Grit does not refer to luck. Grit is also not a short, intense desire. Talent and luck matter to success. But talent and luck do not guarantee grit.

Grit is about having a goal you care about so much that it organises and gives meaning to almost everything you do. Grit is holding steadfast to that goal, even when you fall down, or screw up, or when progress towards that goal halts or slows.

Grit can be measured and, most importantly, practised.

Grit in practice comes down to three ways of thinking:

1. Grit is a habit that can be practised and improved with persistence.
2. Grit is meaningful when it is directed.
3. Grit is a habit that can be supported through community.

This baseline grit mindset will allow you to dive deep into the strategies below and engage with the proposed actions in a more meaningful way.

Strategies to practise grit:

1. Pursue your passion—with focus.
2. Practise deep learning.
3. Share your failures and learn from criticisms.
4. Surround yourself with gritty people.

We will kick off this chapter by getting a better sense of "How gritty are you?"

Find out how gritty you are using the Grit Scale, developed by Duckworth:

	NOT AT ALL	NOT MUCH	SOMEWHAT	MOSTLY	VERY MUCH
New ideas and projects sometimes distract me from previous ones.	5	4	3	2	1
Setbacks don't discourage me. I don't give up easily.	1	2	3	4	5
I often set a goal but later choose to pursue a different one.	5	4	3	2	1
I am a hard worker.	1	2	3	4	5
I have difficulty maintaining my focus on projects that take more than a few months to complete.	5	4	3	2	1
I finish whatever I begin.	1	2	3	4	5
My interests change from year to year.	5	4	3	2	1
I am diligent. I never give up.	1	2	3	4	5
I have been obsessed with a certain idea or project for a short time but later lost interest.	5	4	3	2	1
I have overcome setbacks to conquer an important challenge.	1	2	3	4	5

Source: "Grit Scale," Angela Duckworth, accessed November 4, 2022, https://angeladuckworth.com/grit-scale/.

CALCULATE YOUR SCORE

Add up all the points for the boxes you checked and divide by ten to receive your Grit Score. The maximum score you can achieve is five (extremely gritty), and the lowest score is one (not at all gritty). Use the chart below to see how your score compares to others. (For example, a score of 2.5 reveals that you are grittier than just 10 per cent of the population.)

PERCENTILE	GRIT SCORE
10%	2.5
20%	3.0
30%	3.3
40%	3.5
50%	3.8
60%	3.9
70%	4.1
80%	4.3
90%	4.5
95%	4.7
99%	4.9

Source: "Grit Scale," Angela Duckworth, accessed November 4, 2022, https://angeladuckworth. com/grit-scale/.

REFLECTIVE INQUIRY PRACTICES

- *What does your gritty score say about you?*

- *Do you resonate with the assessment?*
  - *How has this shown up in your personal life?*
  - *How has this shown up in your professional life?*

- *Does your grit manifest differently at work and at home?*

* * *

STRATEGY 1: PURSUE YOUR PASSION—WITH FOCUS

One of the core strategies to practise grit is not just to find one passion and stick with it, but to successfully articulate why that passion is meaningful to you. *How does it speak to who you are, what you believe in, and how that impacts those around you?*

Your reasons do not need to be grand or spectacular. They just need to resonate deeply within you.

This first strategy resonates with my own learning and growth mindset blind spots. Too often, we are passionate about many things, and we divert our attention between multiple passion projects and conversations. Here, we want to differentiate between passion and interest. You can be passionate about a few things but interested in many. The likelihood of superficial engagement and learning increases when your attention is diverted among many interests, even if you possess a talent for those interests.

Talent does not mean grit. In her book, Duckworth uses the following useful equations:

TALENT × EFFORT = SKILL

SKILL × EFFORT = ACHIEVEMENT

In essence, Duckworth's research suggests that when you apply effort to a talent, you gain a skill. When you apply effort to a skill, you gain achievement. In other words, without effort, your talent is just untapped potential. Without effort, your skill is just something you could have done but never did.

That is why grit counts twice—and is such an important factor.

"People that achieve challenging goals stick with their long-term goals instead of getting distracted, and they keep showing up, even when it is difficult," says Duckworth.

Of course, it is important not to get distracted, but realistically, distractions are common. Life happens. I experienced many distractions during my PhD candidacy and along the journey of writing this book. I went through numerous life changes, such as moving to new countries, changing jobs, and having a new baby—not to mention living through an unprecedented global pandemic. I was distracted often, but I always came back to my projects when I was ready. In all instances, pausing my pursuits allowed me to spark new ideas and reflections, which brought new insights and layers to my final outcomes.

What differentiates your grit is that you never really quit. You take a pause. You may even pause often—but you come back to it in light of various distractions.

One of the key differentiators of a gritty person is not that they have blind ambition coupled with stubbornness. More so than not, gritty people are passionate because they find deep meaning in what they do. They are not fuelled by the sense of achievement alone. Gritty people are often moved by the sustainable impact they could make. That could look like a researcher driven to contribute new insights to their field of research or a single parent working multiple jobs to provide for their family. Higher purpose is personal to individuals and does not always need to be a shared vision. However, there are also people who can use their own grittiness to influence the masses. Take, for example, Greta Thunberg, the Swedish environmental activist who, in her relentless pursuit to bring climate change to the forefront of media attention, has inspired younger generations and made climate change sexy again. Even with controversial public figures that we may not resonate with, many have achieved their status through the relentless pursuit of one core belief and message.

The deep connection between you and your passion is what will allow you to practise grit.

What could pursuing passion with focus look like for HR leaders?

This could show up in the way you decide on which part of the HR function you want to excel in or relevant HR-related topics that you would like to be known for as an expert. This may look like you keeping yourself informed with changes and development in that focus area of interest.

Knowing and pursuing your passion as an HR leader means that you will not jump on any interesting new trends and buzzwords, as we often encounter in our profession, and continue to focus on what really matters to you, even if it is not the trendiest topic of the moment.

REFLECTIVE INQUIRY PRACTICES

- *What are you deeply passionate about?*
  - *What was the last time you failed when you did something you were passionate about?*
  - *What did you learn from your failure?*

- *What does your passion mean to you?*
  - *What does your passion mean for others close to you?*

- *How would you describe your passion and its impact in one sentence?*

- *What are your areas of interest?*
  - *Can you articulate how your interests differ from your passion?*

STRATEGY 2: PRACTISE DEEP LEARNING

In addition to connecting with your passion, deep learning will bring your practice of grit to life.

'Deep learning' stemmed from the concept of 'Deep work'. "Deep work" refers to the ability to spend dedicated long and uninterrupted time with complete focus on the task at hand that is challenging or "cognitively demanding," as Cal Newport nicely frames it in his 2013 book *Deep Work: Rules for Focused Success in a Distracted World*. The book discusses the need to master deep work as a skill that allows you to quickly master complicated information and produce better results that also provide the sense of true fulfilment that comes from the ability to master your craft. Newport makes a compelling case for the value of deep work versus shallow work. Newport also elaborates on strategies (what he calls "rules") that teach us to work deeply, embrace boredom, quit social media, and drain the shallows, which are the guiding principles to unlock the values of deep work. Finally, Newport offers practical steps, such as daily scheduling, that are the practices that will form habits that activate the brain and allow us to perform deep work.

Taking inspiration from Newport's thesis, I suggest that the key to cultivating a growth mindset and approaching HR challenges with that mindset is to practise deep learning. I resonate with Newport's thesis that deep work is valuable, rare, and meaningful, and I see the enormous value in channelling the same depth into learning and problem-solving. Combining the idea of the multilayered complexity of the human brain and mind with Newport's deep work thesis, I use the term "deep learning" to describe learning in a focused and uninterrupted manner, similar to how you would approach deep work. The difference between the two is that the outcome of a work product is not as tangible or proactively sought after in deep learning as it is in deep work. Resonating with Newport's reminder of establishing a daily deep work habit, we also anchor deep learning on the requirements to repetitively activate your learning muscles, even in small but concentrated doses. Deep learning is taking your multivitamins in addition to your standard nutrition through three meals. This will be further elaborated in Strategy 3: Schedule and Plan Your Learning Relentlessly.

Deep learning means learning without becoming distracted. Adult learning research shows that the typical learner's attention span wanes after about fifteen to twenty minutes. Surprisingly, that is not much different than an eight-year-old child, whose attention span wanes after sixteen to twenty-four minutes. For reference, a two-year-old child has an attention span of four to six minutes. In our modern world of distractions—smartphones, podcasts, Netflix—the ability to channel one's focus on learning appears to be a greater task than one would expect.

In other words, deep learning is powered by the ability to do deep work.

You may be familiar with the concept of deep learning in the context of machine learning. Deep learning was first introduced as a term that describes a type of machine learning based on artificial neural networks in which multiple layers of processing are used to extract progressively higher-level features from data. Deep learning (also known as deep structured learning) is a subset of machine learning wherein artificial networks and algorithms learn from large amounts of data through machine learning methods. The "deep" in deep learning refers to the use of multiple layers within the network. Having various (deep) layers enables learning in a way that is much like how we humans learn from experience. The deep learning algorithm performs a task repeatedly, each time tweaking it a little to improve the outcome.

"Deep learning" in the context of a growth mindset refers to our ability to explore problem-solving deeply through multiple layers of previous experiences and reflections, as well as by incorporating data derived from questions asked before generating an outcome.

The road to cultivating a growth mindset includes activating curiosity and practising grit through deep learning.

Deep learning is about connecting the dots. It is about asking multiple questions before discovering answers to derive sustainable solutions. It is about forming hypotheses by activating curiosity with practical skills and about looking for data that supports or refutes each hypothesis. Deep learning is also about having the humility to accept that data does not always confirm the hypotheses we like. We must use data to draw insights and to guide us as we explore our contextual realities. We must not be afraid to be wrong in our assumptions. Instead, we must be open to the possibilities of learning—and learning deeply.

What could deep learning and deep thinking look like for HR leaders?

Let us take a practical example. A business leader may come to you as an HR leader and say, "My best performer is going to my competitor for more money. Help!" In this case, the business leader may prefer a best practice mindset and a relatively shallow resolution because it will immediately solve his problem. That may look like a quick counteroffer to keep the employee.

By cultivating a growth mindset through activating curiosity, practising grit, and channelling deep learning, the brain will allow for two things. First, we may consider the best practice, which usually seeks a timely and amicable solution, such as the aforementioned counteroffer to retain the employee. Perhaps there will even be some retention clause attached. But then, the deep-learning and thinking HR professional will start to connect the dots and dive deeper into the issue at hand. People rarely leave just for money. *What is the engagement like in this team? Are there similar patterns with others? What are the macro trends in the industry?*

Deep learning is largely linked to critical thinking, but in the context of HR leaders, critical thinking and deep learning can only add value if the issues people face are resolved in a way that is impactful and sustainable.

Part of deep learning is forming hypotheses and having the curiosity and skills to look for data that provides more insights to support or dismiss that hypothesis. In our example, team engagement data could show there is a systematic retention issue with the team, pointing to a deeper potential issue with the leader and how the team is being managed. Or the performance data could show that the employee has collaboration challenges with colleagues, even if they are a high performer from project deliverable perspective. Regardless of what insights the data may provide, most likely a simple counteroffer will not resolve the issue.

Deep learning allows us to consider issues extensively and provide sustainable solutions rather than quick fixes, which are almost always shallow in nature.

REFLECTIVE INQUIRY PRACTICES

- *Describe the last time you did deep work.*
  - ○ *What were you working on?*
  - ○ *How did that make you feel?*

- *How does the concept of deep learning, as described in this chapter, resonate with you?*

- *Describe the last time you did deep learning.*
  - ○ *What were you learning?*
  - ○ *What was the outcome you were trying to achieve?*
  - ○ *How does deep learning help to achieve the outcome intended?*

STRATEGY 3: SCHEDULE AND PLAN
YOUR LEARNING RELENTLESSLY

"How do you combine full-time work in a senior capacity, a newborn, book writing, and a master's degree all at once?"

Before I answer that in a rather non-spectacular way, I want to highlight that I am not and have never been a gifted person academically. If anything, I failed to thrive in Asia's traditional educational system, where I spent my formative years. To Duckworth's point, success is less about talent or luck than it is about grit. Therefore, the assumption that academic giftedness is the key to multiple project progressions just does not ring true in my case.

To answer the question we started with, other than setting your own expectations and goals high, the most important secret to taking on multiple projects is how you relentlessly schedule your days. This includes the deep learning hours you plan for yourself.

People laugh when they look at my calendar. For starters, it is fully booked—sometimes in fifteen- or thirty-minute blocks. That includes everything from meeting with my CEO to buying socks for my baby. To make it even more entertaining, it is also colour-coded. Each colour is a representation of the role I play, which allows my brain to switch to the right mode as I transition between time blocks. Green means it is a meeting with an external party or blocked out for travel time. Pink signifies regular team meetings. Yellow represents irregular project-related meetings, and blue is blocked for deep learning. Each of these categories requires me to bring different insights and approaches. This colour code is also helpful for context switching and helps me to practise grit in a practical way.

But wait! Before you run off to schedule and pick your favourite colours for team meetings, a helpful discovery process will enable you to consider how you would like to map your schedule and energy. Similar to performance at work, productivity is contextual.

The question is not whether you are a productive person or even how you can become more productive. It is far more impactful to discover *under what context* you are most productive and best able to learn deeply.

What is your preferred learning style?

What time of the day are you naturally more productive?

Once you have a better reflective view of your learning style and time, you can start by blocking out your own deep learning schedule to allow yourself uninterrupted time to research and read. Do not be afraid to go old school. Print out online articles to read on the commute, for example.

The relentless pursuit of learning time is practising grit at its finest.

Keeping a learning journal is also great. It will help you keep your learning habits and process on track, and it will capture thoughts that may be worth returning to. A learning journal does not record progress, but it keeps records of questions and thoughts that we can revisit during our structured learning time. The habit of keeping a learning journal may evolve over time, and there is no one best way to keep one. I used to have multiple handwritten notes, but now I use either my laptop or my phone and add key words more often than full sentences. Occasionally, I take screenshots of electronic materials that I want to refer back to during my structured learning time.

What may scheduling and planning to learn relentlessly look like for HR leaders?

Most of the HR leaders that I know are confined to constant meetings. They are constantly engaged in conversations, whether it is with C-suite leaders they support strategically or the employees that reach out for listening ears. These conversations are not only time-consuming, but they are also energy-consuming. You give a little bit of your soul in every conversation.

Therefore, some of the scheduling of learning and planning may actually be the opposite of having MORE meetings. It may look like being more intentional with the meetings that you are going to take and protecting your energy for scheduled and planned learning.

Therefore, the learning session and timing you schedule for yourself may not be a long stretch, but if they are scheduled and planned with energy preservation in mind, those intentional learning times can be more fruitful.

You are not just scheduling learning for the sake of planning.

REFLECTIVE INQUIRY PRACTICES

- *Explore and discover. What is your most productive time?*
  - *How much of that time could you devote to learning every week?*

- *Start a learning journal.*
  - *What is your preferred way of journalling?*
  - *Why does it speak to you as the preferred method?*
  - *What do you keep track of?*
  - *What have you noticed as a pattern in your learning journal?*

STRATEGY 4: SHARE YOUR FAILURES
AND LEARN FROM CRITICISMS

Success and failure are often treated as binary—opposite sides of the spectrum.

New trends, such as "f**ked-up nights," are becoming a global phenomenon. Instead of groups of people with shared interests getting together to share their successes and what worked for them, as is done at most professional conferences and is the very nature of best practices, people are recognising the power of learning from failure and are getting together to share openly.

To remove sensitivities around failure, people are normalising it by speaking up about it.

Though the tides may be turning, failure and criticism can still be demotivating and ego-threatening. A 2019 study from the University of Chicago suggests that people find failure feedback (criticism) ego-threatening, which leads them to tune out and miss the information the feedback offers. In other words, failure and criticism do not always encourage learning in the utopian way we might hope. The research suggests that halting a pursuit in the moment of failure by tuning out failure feedback could be the first step in a chain reaction that distances and discourages people from the goal they are pursuing. This research is interesting as it points out the role that grit plays in the continuous pursuit of goals despite setbacks, as well as calling out the role that ego plays in learning.

The simple truth is that we need to drop our egos to practise grit.

What could sharing failures and learning from criticisms look like for HR leaders?

As leaders with teams, a practical approach to sharing failures and learning from criticisms is through embedding sharing and learning in team rituals. As busy HR leaders solve people-related issues on the ground, team rituals can often feel daunting and full of transactional details. We often get caught up in the day-to-day manoeuvring of the work and not having the time and space to seek and listen to feedback, nor to share the same attention on providing feedback. Having dedicated time and space in team rituals not only creates a space for such learning to happen, but it also builds the psychological safety of your teams. As self-leaders without teams, these rituals may look internal, where you could capture the learning through the likes of your own learning journal or share it through various domains such as blog posts on LinkedIn or personal blogs.

Sharing your failure is vulnerable. Learning is vulnerable.

REFLECTIVE INQUIRY PRACTICES

- *What did your upbringing teach you about success and failure?*
  - *How have you carried that through your life?*

- *How does failure make you feel?*
  - *When was the last time you shared your failures openly?*
  - *How did that make you feel?*

- *How does criticism make you feel?*

- *What is your first instinct when someone says, "May I share feedback with you?"*

STRATEGY 5: SURROUND YOURSELF
WITH GRITTY PEOPLE

This strategy sounds simple but is perhaps one of the hardest.

Can you name three gritty people in the media? A few names probably roll off the tongue, depending on your industry and exposure. When I asked a few people around me, the popular answers were Steve Jobs, Bill Gates, and Elon Musk. Most believed these people must be gritty to have achieved their success.

On the other hand, when I ask folks to name a few gritty people in their circle of friends, most are silent. That does not mean there are no gritty people around, but we often find "everyday grittiness" hard to define. It is also hard to observe private moments of struggle. Grit is most often associated with struggle, and that can be difficult to see on an individual up and close level.

Indicators of a gritty person are often guided by their overt passion and consistency. They are often the people that consistently stand up for what they believe in and have an infectious nature in our interactions. They may not excel or believe in the same things as you do, but they bring tenacity and consistency in their own viewpoints. They are often not the ones that focus on publicising their struggles or achievement in public forums. My advice for those of you who find it hard to identify gritty people in your own life, I urge you to ask people for their observations. Who do they perceive as gritty and why? And use the responses as a way to reflect.

Everyday grittiness—a daily gritty person—can be felt and observed by those around them. Grit is an infectious energy.

How can we as HR leaders surround ourselves with gritty people?

I love to be introduced to daily gritty people that may not be in my immediate network by asking others to connect me with people with interesting stories. It is a good approach if you are drawing blanks trying to identify daily gritty people around you.

Surrounding ourselves with gritty people does not mean we have to have the same path to life, such as having the same career history or goals of being in HR one way or another. Everyday gritty people are often driven by the changes and impact they have made, regardless of how small, in the areas they are passionate about. Perhaps it is a foreign student learning new languages by practising often in the community, or it may be the shopkeeper down the road that continues to adapt their business in light of Covid restrictions. It may also be parents or grandparents learning to adapt to new technologies.

With their infectious nature, surrounding yourself with gritty people and nurturing these relationships does not require you to be constantly surrounded by them. You can learn from daily gritty people by asking open questions for them to share their experiences and energy with you. My favourite question to ask the gritty people around me is "What have you been up to since the last time we met?" This is often a good trigger question where gritty people will often pause, look me in the eye with a little smile on the edge of their mouth and say, "How much time do we have?"

* * *

Through Part II of this book, I hope that a growth mindset powered by grit is no longer difficult for you to articulate and how it relates to HR leadership, and that HR leader development can be crystallised into action.

Grit is a habit that can be practised and improved with persistence, and that can be supported through partnering with the communities around you. The practical strategies outlined hope to help provide a structured approach for you to practise grit.

Grit can be measured and, most importantly, practised.

PART III

Bringing It All Together

Parts I and II of this book looked at the HR profession at the macro level through the lenses of the industrial revolutions and how following best practices has been a deep-rooted approach for organisations and HR leaders. We bridged the macro understanding and encouraged a much-needed mindset shift by introducing the notion of cultivating a growth mindset through curiosity and grit as the way to break out from the comfort and safe zone of best practices in the context of practising HR. We also walked through clear strategies on how to activate curiosity and practice grit as the cornerstone capabilities.

In Part III and the final chapters of this book, we bring the cultivation of a growth mindset into two frameworks: the HR growth mindset framework, which speaks to the larger HR transformation and capabilities shift at scale, and the **GROWTH** model, which represents the key strategies to activate a growth mindset daily through our approach to problem-solving.

* * *

I remember being in awe of the Ulrich HR competency framework upon first encountering it. I felt both excitement and an overwhelming sense of underachievement. Ulrich and his colleagues suggest there are nine core HR competencies. On top of that, the Results-Based Leadership (RBL) Group's recent research highlights the many hats HR specialists are expected to wear and breaks them into three groups: core drivers, organisation enablers, and delivery enablers. The nine-factor model includes nine roles and twenty-one competencies. The nine roles are strategic positioner, credible activist, paradox navigator, organisation enabler, culture and change champion, human capital curator, and total rewards steward. In other words, as we observe HR research development, we continue to articulate complex and challenging roles that HR leaders are expected to perform to be impactful and strategic.

The questions I find myself asking are these: Is there a world in which, instead of adding more to the plates of existing HR leaders, we re-examine and reimagine the core foundations of HR? Can we pause and ask ourselves, "What is the cornerstone for success?"

Instead of the hyper-specific roles listed above, how about *growth mindset cultivator* and, even more simply, *coach*?

The growth-minded HR framework looks to simplify the understanding of HR competencies powered by the absolute fundamentals that accompany a mindset shift from *what* to *how*.

By this point in the book, you probably already have one phrase scratched into your mind: *a growth mindset is the cultivated product of curiosity and grit.*

Part III of this book brings everything together by providing a framework to articulate how growth-minded HR can be cultivated and practised in a meaningful way in the context of our profession's evolution and our daily work. The framework will include strategies to practise your growth mindset and provide space for curiosity with the reflective inquiry questions you are encouraged to use and continue to revisit as your responses evolve.

CHAPTER 7

Introducing the HR Growth Mindset Framework

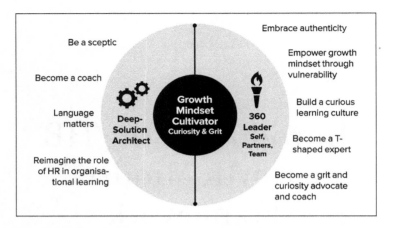

The HR growth mindset framework looks to articulate two fundamental roles of a HR leader: deep-solution architect and 360-degree leader. This framework calls out that the fundamental roles are powered by one core capability: *a growth mindset*, which can be cultivated through activating curiosity and practising grit.

For each of the roles, five growth strategies with practical tactics to enhance HR interactions and outcomes will be shared. We use the term "growth strategies" to mirror the intentions of organisational growth strategies as a plan for overcoming current and future challenges to deliver on their goals for expansion. We also aim to capture the fluid nature of growth—the notion that growth is not one-dimensional nor static.

The simplicity of this framework may seem a little counter-intuitive when compared to some of the more developed HR competency frameworks that have been made popular by researchers, such as the continuously updated Ulrich HR competency model. This framework intends to zoom in on the anchored belief of a growth mindset and cornerstone capabilities for a reimagined HR function, but in no way disregards or discounts the in-depth competency models like the one presented by Ulrich.

This simple model will serve as a practical reference for developing a growth mindset as an HR leader.

* * *

DEEP-SOLUTION ARCHITECT: THE CAPABILITY TO CO-CREATE MEANINGFUL SOLUTIONS WITH YOUR PARTNERS WITHOUT A QUICK FIX OR BEST PRACTICE SOLUTION IN MIND

As a deep-solution architect, the core focus is to deliver impact by providing solutions to people-related problems. These problems can be operational (e.g., how to input data into the employee HR database), tactical on a day-to-day level (e.g., managing individual performance), or strategic (e.g., building a company-wide career architecture to solve the challenges around employee capability development). It is arguable that tactical and strategic problem-solving are the most impactful because they take a sustainable approach to people-related challenges, but we must not overlook the importance of day-to-day problem-solving because that provides the foundation for building trust and partnerships. It is also the baseline for seamless employee and manager experiences. In other words, without tackling the basics of operational problem-solving, it is almost impossible to dive deeper into tactical and strategic problem-solving—or to be invited to the table where major business decisions are made.

Here are five growth strategies to drive impact as a deep-solution architect:

1. Be a sceptic. Assume your first answer is never in-depth enough. Follow the three-questions principle (which I will explain in detail below).
2. Instead of jumping into solutions, become a coach—not a solution executor. Coaching is not a process or an HR intervention; it is a mindset and an approach.
3. Bring consistency through design principles advocacy.
4. Understand the power of language. Be intentional. Remember that language matters.
5. Reimagine the role of HR in organisational learning.

In essence, everything that we need to be an impactful, effective HR solution architect is anchored in problem-solving. Therefore, a growth mindset can be understood as a way of solving problems.

STRATEGY 1: BE A SCEPTIC. ASSUME YOUR FIRST ANSWER IS NEVER IN-DEPTH ENOUGH. FOLLOW THE THREE-QUESTIONS PRINCIPLE.

The term "sceptic" is derived from the Greek *skeptikos*, meaning "to inquire" or "to look around." A sceptic requires additional evidence before accepting claims as the truth. A sceptic is willing to challenge the status quo with open-minded and deep questions. As a deep-solution architect, I want you to be your own sceptic.

Notice when you are leaping towards the first possible solution and question your own thinking by employing the practical tactic that I call the "three-questions principle."

The three-questions principle is simple: Always ask yourself at least three additional questions before offering solutions. Then, ask three more questions after the initial solution is offered. Once an initial solution is derived, the additional three questions should focus on the potential consequences of the solution. I also call this the "triple-three principle". This principle is useful because it provides a practical framework to ensure we do not jump to conclusions or into solution mode when urgent people-related issues are presented.

It may look something like this:

Context: A high performer is leaving. She has an external offer. Her direct manager comes to HR for a solution to retain the employee.

The best practice approach may be to find out what the external offer looks like and try to retain the talent with a competitive counteroffer.

A deep-solution architect powered by a growth mindset using the triple-three principle may look like this:

Before an initial solution is offered, three questions you may want to ask yourself or other relevant leaders are:

1. What are the previous indicators of this employee's intent to leave? Have there been earlier conversations?
2. What is the career development plan for this employee? Does retention serve this purpose in the long run?
3. What is the pattern of departure on this team?

Initial solution proposed by HR: Retain the talent with a counteroffer that is 20 per cent higher than the competing offer. This will result in the employee being paid more than her peers with similar scope and skillsets.

Three questions to ask once the solution is recommended are:

1. Does this serve the retention purpose in the short run?
2. Does the solution offered align with our organisational values, such as fairness? Does this construct an exception in the organisation?
3. How would this affect the remaining team members?

Depending on the answers to these three questions, you may or may not stick to the initial proposed solution. It may turn out that a counteroffer to retain the talent at all costs may cause more challenges (e.g., the morale of the team may be negatively impacted, causing more members to leave) in the near future and that the more sustainable approach is to accept the departure of the employee.

A common objection to this mindful, explorative practice is the misperception of time. I term this a "false urgency" or "self-fulfilling urgency". The false urgency that organisations and leaders often present their problems can cause HR leaders to respond with a best practice and go-to solution to close the loop as soon as possible and move on to the next problem. In reality, with a few exceptions, such as health and safety hazards or a legal compliance breach, most issues do not require an immediate response.

The three-questions principle is a deep practice. It is a lesson in thought processes and deep learning. We must ask questions to learn about issues more deeply and form hypotheses—and also to ensure the solutions we present are multidimensional. Asking questions requires the deep practice of listening, and we must approach answers with an open mind and seek input to modify solutions.

A growth mindset is a brain muscle, and these questions are the exercise that allows you to build and use those muscles. Asking yourself (or your teams) open-ended, exploratory questions allows for engagement in a multidimensional way.

Other reflective questions that may be helpful are:

- *What is the problem we are trying to solve?*
- *How does this solution solve that problem in the short term?*
- *How does this solution solve that problem in the mid to long term?*
- *How may this solution create more problems in the organisation in the future?*

Another practical tactic is to go into a meeting or discussion by thinking through and preparing some questions as part of your triple-three principle. The open-ended questions like the ones above allow both you and the people coming to you with urgent problems the opportunity and space to shift their mindset by changing the narrative from quick-fix answers to deeper questions.

In essence, when we avoid best practices and quick solutions, we allow ourselves to *reconnect* with the problem space. Notice I emphasised the word *reconnect* here. Too often, we think we know the problem we are trying to solve on the surface, and we work towards that without looking deeper, without asking the most important question:

"What is the REAL problem we are trying to solve?"

This question is powerful because (1) it reframes a statement of solution into an open inquiry and (2) it assumes endless possibilities in solving a problem. Questions allow us to understand the *why* behind what we are trying to do, and they become the baseline for thinking about the impact of solving the problem.

Asking questions, however, is often met with backlash for being ineffective in framing problems. Some do not like the negative connotation associated with the word "problem." What I propose is that powerful and direct questions serve as a perspective shift. The effectiveness of a question does not always lie in the answer itself but in its ability to redirect thought processes and allow for new conversations.

As a growth-minded HR, we want to be able to support leaders in thinking through problem spaces before developing solutions.

What I continue to find interesting about being in HR is that many seem to think they can do a much better job without the experience or academic rigour. As I think back on the changes that have happened in HR since the First Industrial Revolution, it never ceases to surprise me that we so gladly accept the changing skillsets and technologies deployed in the sciences and even in entertainment, but we refuse to do the same for HR.

HR remains a profession that is poorly understood and perhaps poorly appreciated in terms of its growth and challenges. This perception is further complicated by the fact that some of the senior HR leaders in the current environment may not have the opportunity to fully experience the changing nature of HR and HR education. Some have moved up from the ranks of HR administration (e.g., they have transitioned from office management to HR management), and some come with the perspective that being in HR means making employees happy and being a likeable person. This serviced-oriented approach to HR does not always set us up to achieve success.

Being in HR is not about being liked. My advice to the next generation of HR professionals—or to those who want to transition into HR—is that the reality of strategic HR is not about being close to people or being a people person. You will never be able to please everyone, and often, you will be the bearer of bad news. You will likely be the face of HR processes and organisational changes that are not appreciated by everyone, and you will constantly struggle to find the right boundaries between relationships and stakeholder management.

Being an impactful deep-solution architect also means having the courage to not be liked.

This backdrop of common misunderstandings can lead to trouble, especially when business leaders often come to HR with a solution already in mind. "I cannot lose this person. Please draft a counteroffer," they might say. Or there might be a natural tendency to ask, "What is the best practice? How does (insert desirable company) do it?" Coupled with the wish to be service-oriented, many HR leaders find themselves becoming the executor of business leaders' requests or the central point for best practice dissemination. The executing mode often taps into our more fixed mindset mentality as we move swiftly into the *doing* rather than the *thinking*.

Therefore, asking yourself and your business leaders "What is the problem we are trying to solve?" is the gateway to reframing and rethinking the problems at hand.

REFLECTIVE INQUIRY PRACTICES

- *Practise the three-questions principle in your upcoming discussions.*
  - *How did it go?*
  - *How did it feel?*

- *Practise asking, "What is the problem we are trying to solve?"*
  - *How did it go?*
  - *How did it feel?*

- *What are three of your go-to questions to expand your practice as a deep-solution architect? Create them and try them out!*
  - *How does it feel?*
  - *What shift can you observe from those you are co-creating the solution with?*
  - *What shifts can you observe for yourself?*

* * *

STRATEGY 2: BECOME A COACH—NOT A SOLUTION EXECUTOR. COACHING IS NOT A PROCESS OR AN HR INTERVENTION. IT IS A MINDSET AND AN APPROACH.

As I continue to grow in my career, I have started to reflect on how having all the answers—or even being perceived as having all the right answers—is a dangerous and slippery slope. It used to feel empowering to know the answers (or be perceived that way), and it continued to power my career growth in HR. But the bigger the scope and responsibilities, the more complex the problems and the more the best practice approach feels superficial and flat. In best-case scenarios, taking a best practice approach means that leaders rely on and come to you for issues. In worst-case scenarios, however, you become the type of HR leader who provides standard, textbook answers that do not capture the context and nuance of the situations you are tasked with solving. Perhaps worst of all, you are not enabling employees and leaders to tap into their own internal thought process and infinite learning capacities.

One of the worst outcomes of a best practice mindset and approach is when it limits the opportunity for yourself and others to activate and develop your own growth mindset. I want to reimagine a world where HR leaders are deep-solution architects that work together with business leaders to build solutions that are meaningful and impactful through coaching.

A rather formal definition accepted academically is that workplace coaching is "a one-to-one, custom-tailored learning and development intervention that uses a collaborative, reflective, goal-focused relationship to achieve professional outcomes that are valued by the coachee." According to the International Coach Federation—a professional coaching governance body—

coaching is a learning and development approach that places the learner at the centre of the learning experience. The popularity of coaching appears to be enduring, with an estimated 53,300 professional coaches operating at present.

Coaching as a performance or behavioural intervention approach is widely accepted in many parts of Asia. As HR leaders, we usually think about coaching in the context of employee learning and development or as a way to cultivate effective leadership. We will likely introduce coaching as an intervention for a leader who needs some leadership behavioural coaching or as part of a talent development initiative for employees with high potential as part of a succession planning process. Still, this approach to coaching often lacks the fundamental depth required to embrace coaching holistically as a development and organisational culture approach and not a standalone intervention activity.

As deep-solution architects, we must embrace coaching as a mindset and as an approach to problem-solving.

This fundamental shift in mindset supports the growth and development of individuals from a reflective and introspective point of view, extending the influence of coaching from the self to the broader contexts that we operate in, whether that is personal or professional. Coaching embraces the mindset of curiosity through insightful questions—not best practices.

I advocate for coaching to become a mindset and a way of engaging with your internal stakeholders, regardless of the population (i.e., employees or leaders) or hierarchy, from the CEO down to first-time people managers. I suggest coaching as a way for HR professionals to drive meaningful conversations and speak to the growth mindset of HR.

What does meaningful coaching in the moment of a consequential and productive conversation among people look like? It looks like a burst of curiosity and energy. The conversation is about asking inquisitive questions, with the assumption that there is always a deeper layer to the issue at hand. It feels like a discovery experience, where problems are being unpacked without a preconceived notion of what the correct outcome might be.

Coaching may not always be activated through questions.

Sometimes in my conversations, I feel like I need much more information or even just some space to think. I can sense a brick wall building between myself and the person talking to me, likely because they are in solution mode and not open to being questioned. In these cases, I use two powerful *probing requests*:

"Walk me through your thought process."

This is a powerful probing request because it shifts the focus from needing to solve the problem to listening to another person. This is a great one to use when you are in a scenario where the other person brings forth a solution to a problem that you may not agree with. Instead of jumping into disagreement and presenting alternative solutions, this is a great way to unpack the baseline values driving the other person's decision-making framework. By understanding that, you may be able to craft a solution together that is aligned with both your values and thinking.

"Tell me more."

This probing request is impactful even though it comes packaged in so few words because it opens the door for a perspective to be deepened and allows the other person—typically the one who comes to you with an issue that needs solving—an open space to share their thoughts without needing to justify them.

The one question and one probing statement technique may look like this:

- What is the problem we are trying to solve?
  - Tell me more.
- How does this connect to the problem we are trying to solve?
  - Walk me through your thought process.

Strive for a coaching conversation to be a two-way conversation. A simple technique that I use to activate a coaching conversation is the *one question and one probing request technique*. Taking the same scenario of "My high performer has received another offer. I would like to counteroffer" from above, the one question you may ask is "Was this a surprise to you?" and the probing request could be "Tell me more." The shift from "I want to have a counteroffer" to "Let us walk down memory lane" is often helpful to break leaders from reaction mode to reflection mode.

Coaching is not about getting to an answer but creating the path for co-creating an impactful solution.

REFLECTIVE INQUIRY PRACTICES

- *On a scale of one to ten (ten being the highest), how comfortable are you with not having all the right answers at your immediate disposal?*

- *What is your perception of coaching?*

- *Practise the one question and one probing statement technique.*
  - *How did it go?*
  - *How did it make you feel?*
  - *What are some probing statements that are powerful for you?*

STRATEGY 3: BRING CONSISTENCY THROUGH DESIGN PRINCIPLES ADVOCACY.

As a deep-solution architect, the need to bring consistency in the depth of thinking and solution design becomes a critical part of how those working with you experience their interactions with you.

Consistency can be particularly challenging as HR leaders often have to navigate the paradox of policy alignment (i.e., a remote work policy and compensation bands), which is often met with the request for policy exception for circumstances that may be perceived as unique and urgent.

Design principles are a set of considerations that form the basis of any good product and are often used in the context of good product design. For example, the design principles of AirBnB were unified (no isolated features), universal (welcoming and accessible), iconic (bold design and functionality), and conversational (easily understood by users). These four design principles help AirBnB make the right trade-offs and, most importantly, be consistent with their products.

In organisational settings, design principles can also manifest in terms of organisational values or leadership principles. Amazon, for example, popularly emphasises fourteen leadership principles: customer obsession; ownership; invent and simplify; are right, a lot; learn and be curious; hire and develop the best; insist on the highest standards; think big; bias for action; frugality; earn trust; dive deep; have backbone, disagree, and commit; and deliver results. These principles are used to establish consistent expectations for leaders in Amazon.

Design principles help teams with decision-making and bring consistency and fairness in decision outcomes. A few simple principles or constructive questions will guide your team towards making appropriate decisions that often feel difficult and uncomfortable. I love to see HR leaders use the same approach when designing organisational solutions, regardless of if they are big or small.

A practical tactic to practise bringing consistency through design principles in your interactions as an HR leader is to bridge and agree with leaders on what those design principles look like before jumping into providing a solution. Design principle advocacy may look much subtler, and the words "design" or "principle" may never be used. The key is to think about making difficult decisions and defusing emotional reactions that people often come to you with through a mutual anchor of consistent principles.

Useful questions include:

- *What are some of the principles we do not want to deviate from?*
- *What are our non-negotiables?*
- *What is important to you?*
- *What do you want this decision to convey about your leadership?*

I remember getting into a heated discussion with a leader who wanted one of his team members to go on performance management due to "insubordination." When I asked the leader to elaborate on what happened, he shared that he made a decision that his team disagreed with, and they went behind his back to other leaders to find advocacy for the opposite. In his mind, the solution to this problem was a PIP, and I was expected to execute it promptly.

I listened, paused, and then I asked: "What is important for you as a leader?" He was still a little emotional and hurt from what he felt was insubordination from his team.

"I believe in fighting for what is right and that hierarchy does not matter. I believe that I set a good example for my team," he said.

"Walk me through the last time you challenged your manager's decision" was my response. Now it was his turn to pause.

The leader agreed that what he wanted consistently in his leadership was to focus on championing good ideas, even if that meant going against the tides. He agreed to speak with the person again and find a middle ground on the earlier decision based on the understanding of why other leaders are supportive of this idea. By the end of the conversation, we agreed on a set of simple leadership principles for this team, which we continue to use for recruitment development and performance review to capture consistency.

Design principles help us co-create solutions with leaders and frame decision buy-in with consistency and fairness.

REFLECTIVE INQUIRY PRACTICES

- *What are your personal life design principles?*
  - *How do you channel them to make life decisions?*

- *What are some product or organisational design principles that resonate with you?*
  - *What do you like about them?*
  - *What do you not like about them?*

- *How do you channel design principles in your work?*

STRATEGY 4: BE INTENTIONAL. LANGUAGE MATTERS.

This may feel intuitive, but many of us forget it when we get into the weeds of things. We catch ourselves using terms like "best practices," "policy," "process governance," and "playbook" as a way to communicate credibility and structural thought processes. Most of all, we use this language as a safety net when facing objections, especially when combating negative sentiments from business leaders on HQ-owned, HR-related decisions that may be made independent of regional or local offices. This is particularly prevalent in Asia, where many of the MNC HQs are outside of Asia.

When we communicate the restrictions of policies, which is often the starting point of tension between the business and HR, how do we refrain from the helpless language of "This global policy is out of my hands" and instead transition to "How do we make this policy work for our context?"

Case in point: as working conditions and expectations continue to evolve because of the global pandemic, pre-existing HR policies and practices are often under the microscope. For example, in a company that expects employees to return to the office, how do we navigate situations where employees do not want to return? How do we communicate beyond the policy of *how* (i.e., policy dictates your team must return to the office) to communicate the *why* (i.e., the dynamics of innovation) and later find a *how* (i.e., what are the obstacles to returning to the office safely, and how can we best remove them?) that connects to the sustainability of the team and the organisation.

As deep-solution architects, we must be intentional in how we communicate our approaches and outcomes. We *must* be intentional.

Language also matters when it comes to how we communicate our roles and impact. Much critical language research suggests that linguistic power can be observed on multiple levels. At the macro level, language is a collective identity shared by a community. In this case, the community is us, the HR leaders who speak the language of HR in ways that communicate both intent and, most importantly, our approach to solving people-related issues and challenges. At the micro level, language reveals the speaker's influence and status or, on the flip side, a lack of it.

Language is for communication, and it reflects power dynamics.

One thing that hit me strongly when I started working in Indonesia was the use of the term "user" to describe business leaders with whom we were interfacing. This was the first time I became acutely aware of the power of language in relation to the power dynamics that exist between HR and its respective business in an emerging market. These power dynamics are still prevalent today. In the West, it is more common to refer to these people as "business leaders" or even just "the business." When my Indonesian HR team referred to the business as "the user," it initially struck me as a reflection of a deeply unsettling imbalance of power.

"My users think the performance management timeline is unrealistic," they would say.

Paying attention to language and how it conveys power dynamics is critical. The use of the word "user" implies a few things. For one, it suggests that HR is a service that a consumer or customer pays to use, which shifts the dynamic from partnership to consumership, wherein the decision power ultimately sits with the customer. Second, it does not capture the capabilities expected of HR leaders. It reflects the use of HR services as a *thing*, like a username for a computer domain or a user of a good, rather than recognising the dynamic and challenging skillset required to be impactful business partners. Lastly, it builds on and continues to perpetuate through language the historical power dimensions between different job functions.

As I mentioned at the start of this book, we often think of ways to transform the way *to do HR*. "Doing HR" communicates that HR is inherently understood as an activity rather than a practice or a highly skilled profession that works with complex people-related issues.

A practical tactic to reassess the language you use on a daily basis is to ask yourself what those words look like independent of the context. Ask yourself, how is the word being used in other settings, and what does it communicate? Consider the term "user"—how is it used in other settings? Are you the user of certain goods and services? What does that language convey?

Language and what it conveys is contextual and very much embedded in the cultural and organisational dimensions, but as companies become more global and as teams become less restricted to geographical boundaries, HR leaders must ask: *how can we be more intentional in our communication by paying attention to the language we use?*

REFLECTIVE INQUIRY PRACTICES

- *Describe a time when the language you used may have been counterproductive in your work as an HR leader.*
  - *What could be done differently?*
  - *Was it just about the words? What did these words represent, or what emotions did it trigger for you and those you were communicating with?*

- *On a scale of one to ten (ten being the highest), how would you describe the power dynamics between the business and the HR department where you work?*
  - *How does the language you use day to day contribute to that?*
  - *What is one word/term that you would like to see change in your current context?*
  - *What are the steps you can take to start changing the association with the word used?*

STRATEGY 5: REIMAGINE THE ROLE OF HR IN ORGANISATIONAL LEARNING.

If curiosity, not skill, is the problem, then the way organisations think about talent development must fundamentally change. I am parking this strategy under the solution-architect part of the framework, as organisational development remains a core challenge for which organisational leaders expect HR to drive and influence outcomes.

Many organisations currently take a more programmatic approach to learning. We start with a series of learning objectives, come up with a curriculum, and create a bunch of content to impart the skills we think our employees need. But what if we could teach employees a skill that encourages them to pick up other skills on their own?

What if all we need to teach employees is simply how to learn and be curious?

Changing the way employees learn also means changing the way we measure learning. Most learning key performance indicators currently reflect a very transactional approach to learning. We track things like the percentage of course completion, employees' satisfaction rates, or the scores on pop quizzes. What we do not track is whether these courses have activated employees to dive deeper into the topic of interest. If employees pick up a course at work on topic A, are they curious enough to look up related topics B, C, and D?

Transforming the organisational approach to talent development will require going back to the fundamental psychology and methodologies behind learning.

I particularly like the Montessori approach to early childhood education. Dr. Maria Montessori (1870–1952) was an Italian physician and anthropologist who, by scientifically observing children all over the world, discovered universal patterns of development regardless of culture and era. She distilled her findings into a method of education for children up to fifteen years old that is based on self-directed activity, hands-on learning, and collaborative play. Montessori classrooms are thoughtfully designed environments where every material supports an aspect of child development. Children can respond at any moment to natural curiosity in the classroom, building the foundation for lifelong learning.

How can we, as organisations, reactivate our employees' sense of curiosity?

In a 2018 Merck curiosity report, 64 percent of the 3,000 employees surveyed across multiple countries and industries identified that the biggest barrier to curiosity and innovation in the working environment is the top-down approach to organisational learning and working initiatives. The top-down approach means that the employee input is minimal. The research concluded that innovation has not yet really become an established feature of corporate culture and that the curiosity potential of company employees is not being harvested.

As deep-solution architects, HR leaders must guide the organisation towards a different way to learn, foster, and reward curiosity.

Many of us start our lives curious. Toddlers pick things up, smell them, and put them in their mouths, but many of us lose that sense of curiosity along the way.

How can we, as organisations, reactivate our employees' sense of curiosity?

How can we combine our scientific knowledge of learning, such as Montessori's methodology, with practical applications in the workplace to transform the way we develop our talent?

It is difficult to articulate practical tactics for this strategy because it requires us to reimagine the work we do, and that requires a collective mindset shift. As deep-solution architects, we must acknowledge the role of learning in the way we think through and provide guidance on organisational and people solutions.

One practical tactic that I can introduce here is to encourage you to have learning in the back of your mind to elevate discussions and start introducing the term "curiosity" into your daily vocabulary. Make the exploration of curiosity in your organisation a common baseline. Ask: how can we actively remove barriers to curiosity at work?

Can you find ways to reframe your discussions with curiosity as an anchor?

REFLECTIVE INQUIRY PRACTICES

- *How would you articulate the learning culture in your organisation?*
  - *How does it manifest?*

- *What is the role of HR in your organisational learning?*

- *What does learning mean to you?*

- *How can we activate learning in ways that are not programmatic in nature?*

- *What are your current barriers to curiosity?*
  - *How can we actively remove barriers to curiosity?*

- *What are the current barriers to curiosity in your work?*
  - *How can we actively remove barriers to curiosity?*

- *What is an example where you reframe your discussions with curiosity as an anchor?*

360-DEGREE LEADER: THE CAPACITY TO UNDERSTAND COMPLEX LEADERSHIP THAT EMBRACES COLLABORATION AND ACTIVATION OF THE SELF, PARTNERS, AND TEAMS

As noted earlier, the 360-degree experience of leadership considers four key elements: *the self, internal partners, external partners,* and *the team.* Although it is not uncommon to see senior HR leaders serving in organisations without a team in the conventional direct reporting sense, we may consider "the team" to refer to the ability to provide leadership to internal clients as well as leading self.

Some of the strategies outlined below may appear generic, but when you apply them to your own unique HR leadership setting, they may provide a worthwhile lens.

Here are five growth strategies to drive impact as a 360-degree leader:

1. Embrace authenticity.
2. Empower a growth mindset though vulnerability.
3. Build a curious learning culture with intent.
4. Become a T-shaped expert.
5. Become a grit advocate and coach for your team.

STRATEGY 1: EMBRACE YOUR AUTHENTICITY

Authenticity feels very fluffy and unconstructive as a point of reference. In the context of a growth mindset, however, authenticity is about reflecting on what specific circumstances bring out the best learner in you and, on the flip side, knowing which environments do not always empower you to be the best leader.

Such reflections require humility and an appreciation for what works for you and what does not. Authenticity is also a two-way street; it is about appreciating the power of our differences and about having the cultural intelligence to recognise that our different perspectives may allow for stronger and more impactful organisational solutions.

I use three critical elements to define authenticity:

1. Being true to who we are and our values.
2. Understanding our impact on the people around us.
3. Embracing the fact that we do not know the answer to everything and that we are not always right.

What *is not* authentic leadership? Authentic leadership can seem a bit nebulous. Sometimes, it helps to understand a concept by understanding what it is not. Authentic leadership is not an excuse to limit our need to change. We all have areas where we can grow. Authentic leadership is also not an excuse to act like a jerk or to treat people poorly or disrespectfully. I am often shocked by the vast number of senior leaders who behave poorly and use authentic leadership as the shield for such behaviour. Authenticity is not an excuse to express unfiltered thoughts and emotions or to act offensively, rudely, or in other inconsiderate ways towards employees. It is also not an excuse to overshare or to blur boundaries between leaders and their team members.

Yelling at your team members is not practising authenticity. Yelling at your team members is not acceptable, and it never will be.

Authenticity does not equal narcissism. It is not about being an unfiltered self but about being a conscientious leader who understands your impact on others. During many of my executive coaching sessions, I have heard business and HR leaders express sentiments like, "This is just me, and I am just being authentic!" in response to criticisms of their leadership, following times when they may have lost their temper at work or used inappropriate language. When I hear this response, I often remind managers or leaders of the three critical elements that define authenticity. I encourage them to reconnect to their own personal values and how those values impact others. For instance, their personal value could be that no time should be wasted, which translates into impatient criticism of their team members. Without sacrificing one's leadership value, it is important to consider how that value impacts others. Despite the media hype on the "genius a**hole" narcissistic startup leadership culture, that is not authentic leadership in practice.

On the other end of the spectrum, if you are powered by the need to be liked as a leader, it is easy to start blurring boundaries between you and your team members, especially in a family-oriented organisational culture. It fuels the challenging behaviour of making decisions that may not take the big picture of team fairness and organisational consistency in mind. For instance, making compensation decisions based on personal needs rather than job scope and skills proficiency.

Authenticity is also not an excuse for not performing at the level that is expected of you in your role, nor is it a reason to not mitigate activities at which you do not excel. Authenticity requires you to have insights into your strength and opportunity for growth and to understand what your operating contexts require from you and how to adapt towards that without shifting your whole being. I once worked with a leader that did not excel in public speaking. He did not enjoy team townhalls, and he often tripped on his own words or cracked jokes that did not always translate in a cross-cultural team across the Asia region.

This organisation was going through fundamental HR and business transformations, where a highly motivating and inspirational senior HR leader was required. Many of his team members shared feedback on his public speaking performance, and he admitted that he is better in one-on-one settings and that the joke-cracking in townhall was a way for him to calm his nerves. However, even with that realisation, he decided to not prioritise one-on-one meetings to reconnect and motivate his teams in ways he knows he is more effective and is required given the organisational context, albeit the competing priorities.

This leader prioritised managing above his hierarchy rather than his team. Within twelve months, there was a 50 percent turnover on his team because he refused to recognise his own development needs and did not meet the leadership needs of the organisation.

Being an authentic leader, either of a team or just of yourself, allows you to explore how to maximise impact. Becoming an authentic leader means listening, asking questions, remaining humble, and being willing to examine your failures. We can achieve this when we embrace vulnerability. Vulnerability is the ability to ask for help when it is needed, to humbly listen to the responses we receive, and, when necessary, to examine our failures. Authentic leaders are not ashamed when they do not know everything. This is an important distinction, especially for leaders coming from outside of Asia, where many things are different. The truth is we do not know everything. For those of us who have worked in mature markets, emerging markets are truly foreign to us and the ways we have been taught to do business. Even amid the same emerging Asian market, the countries we operate in—and thus the worlds we inhabit—can be vastly different. We need to be able to admit that we do not always know the answers.

What does it mean to be true to your own values and self in an emerging market? The growth environment in such markets often brings challenges to personal ethics and values. What may be true in a mature market is often not the case in an emerging one. Therefore, how you manoeuvre within that fluid line is the key to success.

Understanding your impact on others, whether on a cultural or practical level, is the key to connecting with your teams in emerging markets. Due to power distances, as a senior leader, you are someone who is perceived as hard to reach, yet you have a profound, direct impact on employees' everyday work lives.

I learnt this first-hand on one of my first business trips when I began working in Indonesia as the chief HR officer. In that organisation, when we travelled, different management levels stayed in different hotels based on different budgets. On one particular trip, my hotel was about a forty-five-minute drive from the airport, while some of my more junior team member's hotel was about a fifteen- or twenty-minute drive. Because of seniority, I was always given a driver, while my team took a taxi. On one occasion, we were all travelling together. I knew that my team's hotel was on the way to my hotel, so I offered to give them a ride. The team seemed uncomfortable with my offer, but they were nevertheless very polite and accepted it. About twenty-five minutes into the ride, I noticed we had yet to arrive at my team's hotel, so I asked the driver why we were not there yet. Much to my shock, I discovered that because I was the senior officer in the car, the driver had to drop me off first. And because of Indonesian culture, no one on my team was going to speak up about it. I thought I was doing them a favour by dropping them off on the way, but instead, I ended up extending their trip by over an hour.

Authentic leadership means we add value through the lens of our team's experiences and not what we perceive as value-adding.

The story of the Indonesia car rides stays with me throughout my career. I should have asked what would be helpful for the team in terms of getting back to their hotel. It is about asking questions rather than assuming the answer. I should have activated more curiosity, especially within a new culture and working with new teams. What may be perceived as valuable for me may not be the case for others.

Authenticity is a choice on how you add value as a leader every day.

Authenticity means have the awareness and courage to ask:

"How can I be helpful to you?"

REFLECTIVE INQUIRY PRACTICES

- *Articulate your authentic self as a leader.*
  - *When are you at your best?*
  - *When are you at your worst?*
  - *How do they manifest in your behaviour?*

- *Ask your team member and/or business leader that you partner with to describe your leadership style and personal value*
  - *Does it resonate?*
  - *Are they aligned in their perceptions?*
  - *Why or why not?*

STRATEGY 2: EMPOWER A GROWTH MINDSET THROUGH VULNERABILITY

Embracing that we do not know the answer to everything and are not always right is a large part of developing a growth mindset through vulnerability.

It is okay for us not to know everything. Opening ourselves up to vulnerability and curiosity is the growth mindset in practice.

Authentic leaders who embrace vulnerability will hold their teams in high regard. They value the contributions that each member brings. The leader's job is to help their team connect the knowledge and experience the leader brings with the knowledge and experience the team brings—on such topics as culture, government regulations, the external environment, and more. This shared knowledge, when brought together, creates a powerful partnership. When you work towards a solution via a partnership, regardless of whether that idea fails or succeeds, you have created an environment that will drive real, long-lasting results.

When we approach our teams from a place of authenticity, we can shine a light on their untapped potential.

Authentic leaders value winning together.

Imagine how it would feel to be asked, *"What do you think?"* when you have never been asked that before. This is the experience for many of our employees in emerging Asia. This one question is powerful, whether you are leading an HR team or working with talent in other divisions and departments. That one question goes a long way towards fostering engagement, loyalty, and retention, and it can help you to generate better results by generating better solutions.

One of the key challenges for me coming into an emerging market was to connect reward strategies to reality. Moving from a market in which the average salary a month is $3,000 to an environment where the average monthly salary could be as low as $300 was challenging for me to embrace. When planning for a rewards system review, instead of relying on what I knew as a best practice, I simply asked my teams to share with me their thoughts and recommendations as a starting point for a discussion on rewards.

"What do you think?" I once asked the payroll manager about salary reviews. I will always remember the semi-panic and shock that ran through her eyes. She was silent and then finally

gave a tentative response: "Are you asking me what I think? No one has ever asked me that." This was a powerful reminder for me as an authentic leader that the ability to create a safe space for others to think and be agile is the key to succeeding in emerging markets.

The friction between a best practice mindset and a growth mindset leadership can be visible at all levels of seniority. When I was working at an Indonesian healthcare organisation, we hired a new marketing director who had previously worked in the aviation industry. In an industry like aviation, best practices around health and safety are a *necessity*, and fostering a safety culture is imperative. There are few ways to adapt or evolve those practices, and there is not much need to do so.

For a healthcare organisation in an emerging market, the opportunities to reconsider best practices and build growth practices in marketing were limitless. There was just one problem: the marketing director was stuck in a best practice mindset. Immediately upon his arrival, he recommended the organisation spend millions of dollars on a massive billboard campaign focused on brand loyalty. It was a good strategy for a national airline trying to attract a mass-market or a middle-class air traveller. But this was a healthcare organisation composed of community pharmacists serving the emerging middle class. Its customers were not the ones who would look at the shiny billboard and think, "I am going to go to the pharmacy because they can take care of my health." The core mission and vision of the organisation was to make people live longer and healthier lives. Its customers were driven to its pharmacies because they had chronic conditions like diabetes that they wanted help treating. What the potential customers needed to know is that we cared about what they care the most about, which is health, and we are here to help by making chronic disease care more accessible to all.

Healthcare in Indonesia is about caring for people in need, but the marketing director missed this point—and so did the marketing campaign. In the end, the healthcare organisation wasted time and money on an unsuccessful billboard campaign that only served to distract them from reaching the right customers with their core mission and vision. The marketing director committed a common mistake: he took a best practice that had worked in his previous industry and superimposed it onto his new industry in a different market, expecting the same results.

To succeed in emerging Asia, HR leaders and senior business leaders need the strength—and courage—to recognise that what they have been taught about best practices may, in fact, not be the best. They need the strength and courage to speak out and say, "Let us try something else." However, they cannot simply state that a best practice will not work; they have to provide alternative recommendations for the organisation to try. This requires calculated risks to come up with innovative solutions. He left the organisation within a few months due to poor cultural fit.

Agile thinking is a powerful tool. But agile thinking combined with authentic leadership is exponentially more powerful. Agility, in fact, has been found to be linked to authenticity and authentic leadership. Emerging markets change rapidly, so we have to think and execute quickly. At the same time, management in emerging markets is much more visible and connected to the people than we often see in mature markets, so how we as leaders conduct ourselves is crucial to our impact.

Being a vulnerable leader also means listening and accepting the impact you have on others and acting on the constructive criticism you receive. I have been confronted a few times in my career with the claim that I was not stepping up to the expectations of my teams. I was once called out for travelling too much and leading the team from a bird's-eye view and the status quo rather than providing thoughtful leadership and connecting with the team as individuals. I was given a firm and clear message by my senior leadership team that my team of twenty-five was dissatisfied with how I was managing them. I recall a sense of natural defensiveness. I felt unappreciated. At the time, I was heading three departments with a total of forty-five team members—and the complaining team was only one of many hats I had to juggle. I felt misunderstood and frustrated and, worse, a little attacked by those who were supposed to be on my side.

Being a vulnerable leader does not mean that you are a saint. It means that you are hyper-aware of how you are feeling and how others are feeling. Give yourself permission to feel attacked, hurt, or misunderstood during the initial phase of criticism. It is how you channel your energy after digesting and learning from the constructive feedback that matters.

After working through my initial emotions, I was able to reflect on the three gaps that I needed to close as a leader:

1. Strategic and informational transparency. How do I help the team understand what they do and how they connect with each other?

2. Connecting with team members as individuals and as a collective.
3. Providing access points during challenging schedules.

Such reflections led to drastic key actions that were instituted consistently and without fail:

1. I arranged strategic team sessions to clearly articulate the meaning of the work that we do. I also drafted and sent a weekly note to update the team on the progress of our strategic intent and to provide transparency across teams.
2. I held weekly team meetings that focused on getting to know each other and having fun as a team—with themes like dressing up as your favourite TV character.
3. I blocked off and opened a weekly three-hour walk-in session for the team to connect with me without a prior appointment. This could be in-person or through virtual engagement, such as phone calls and Slack. I committed to a ten minute response time during the block off time.

After six months of consistent execution of the tactical engagements listed above, this team was highlighted with the highest engagement and retention through the annual engagement survey and 360-degree leadership reports.

I have learnt—and continue to learn—through the experiences and observations shared that it is important to make peace with imperfections and live with vulnerability. Through multiple career moves and a focus on transformation, I am sometimes successful in my adventures—and sometimes not so much. Each of my successes and failures is a learning opportunity worth reflecting on.

Being intentional with sharing your vulnerability will reinforce your authenticity.

REFLECTIVE INQUIRY PRACTICES

- *What is the one core principle/value you stand by in life?*

- *Invite someone who is close to you professionally to share their observations of your authenticity.*
  - *Does it resonate?*
  - *How does it feel to ask someone to share their observations of you?*

- *How do you usually react when someone criticises your work?*
  - *Does this align with how you think you should react?*

- *When was the last time you asked, "What do you think?" to your team or to others with opposing views?*
  - *What was that experience like?*

STRATEGY 3: BECOMING A T-SHAPED EXPERT

Going beyond a single industry focus is the key to becoming a "T-shaped expert." A T-shaped expert refers to an individual who is capable in many areas but also is an expert in at least one specialisation. This contrasts with an "I-shaped expert," who has deep expertise in one area, or a "horizontal generalist," who is capable in many areas but is not an expert in any of them. In the context of HR, an I-shaped expert is usually found in the space of Centre of Expertise/Excellence (COE), such as compensation and benefits specialists. HR business partners are often viewed as the horizontal generalists that understand the intricacy and interconnectedness of the various elements of HR capabilities.

The concept of expertise can also be applied through the lens of industry focus as an HR leader. There absolutely is value in staying within a single industry of interest and becoming an expert within that industry. It is common to see strong HR professionals with singular industry exposure in the financial and technology sectors.

Becoming a multi-industry expert as a T-shaped HR leader requires intentionality and agility, fuelled by a growth mindset. Recognising that becoming a "T-shaped HR leader" describes a destination, Scott Ambler and Mark Lines, the authors of *Choose Your WoW!: A Disciplined Agile Delivery Handbook for Optimising Your Way of Working*, suggest that "generalising specialists" is the term to describe the journey. For us, the journey is described as part of being a growth-minded T-shape expert that embraces human adaptability.

Being a 360-degree leader also means that you have the capacity to look beyond the specialised understanding you have and be willing to explore the multidimensional HR profession that crosses industries, organisational size, and HR specialisation. I have observed this deep sense of requirement as HR leaders advance in their careers. Three of the biggest reflective questions for HR leaders when they are faced with career transition opportunities or pathways are (1) whether they should stay and become industry experts and grow their careers alongside a changing and evolving industry (such as high-tech, startup, or financial industries), (2) whether they should pursue a role as a generalist (i.e., HR director across all HR functional specialisations, or as functional or business line HRBPs), or (3) whether they should become a specialist (i.e., working in COE-type roles with one pillar focus).

The short answer from me is always to try them all!

The long answer is coming, but in essence, the choice is not black and white. If anything, you are able to plan out a diverse HR career without feeling the need to pick one over another, as long a growth mindset anchors your career decisions. Tactically, what this means is that in each career move, the key question that you are going to ask is no longer vertically directed, such as "Am I getting a bigger title?" or "Is the salary better?" Instead, the biggest question you are going to ask with every move becomes:

"What do I want to learn? How would investing in change support my growth?"

Too often, we think about career growth in a vertical manner. We are always searching for the next bigger and better paying job. Reflecting on my own career, I was able to grow into my current state of career by taking the deliberate and non-conventional route of making multiple horizontal (and at times lower-salaried) career moves and being exposed to many different industries and countries. I have learnt and grown as an HR specialist and as an HR strategist and generalist across six industries and four countries to date.

As I reflect back on the path I took, I notice a few turning points.

At twenty-four, I was working in the hospitality industry, but I turned down the offer to become the regional HR head following an acquisition because I recognised the need to continue learning and growing my HR technical skills in knowledge-intensive industries. With that in mind, I took a more junior HR management position with a newly merged Norwegian state oil organisation and relocated from London to Norway. Because of that move, I had the opportunity to learn and adopt a structured approach in an established HR environment.

At twenty-seven, I relocated to Singapore to take on a role as head of HR in an emerging market instead of continuing to grow in a larger and more established HQ. Through this move, I learnt to scale HR practices and lead HR transformation across geographies and as a country HR lead.

At thirty-one, I relocated to Indonesia without prior networks, friends, or family. This move allowed me to learn C-level HR partnership and be hands-on in driving social impact through COE functions such as learning and business model transformation, as well as learning to make impact as regional HRBP head with a regional expansion focus.

At thirty-six, I entered a brand-new industry—gaming and entertainment. This move allowed me to learn a brand new and thriving industry while continuing to practise as an HR business partner and build and lead a team across Asia.

Examining each potential career move through the lens of what I want to learn and what I can contribute has allowed me to continue to grow and make career changing decisions. As my experience illustrates, career growth is not always represented by bigger titles and more money. I have taken at least three pay cuts and two title drops to move into new roles and learn new things. While this did not necessarily contribute to my vertical growth, it allowed me to learn from each role. It can be good to take a step back and look at growing horizontally in your career.

Becoming a T-shaped expert does not mean you have to be good at everything. Instead, it calls you to focus on your strengths and to do more than enough to make sure your weakness does not become your obstacle to success.

REFLECTIVE INQUIRY PRACTICES

- *What do your current career trajectories say about your current expertise?*
  - *What shape of an expert are you?*
  - *Does this career narrative resonate with you?*

- *What could being a T-shaped HR leader look like for you?*
  - *What area of HR interests you to dive deeper into?*

- *What do you need to do to develop that expertise?*

STRATEGY 4: BUILD A CURIOUS LEARNING CULTURE WITH INTENTION

As people leaders in pursuit of a growth mindset, we have the responsibility and accountability to develop the next generation of HR professionals and leaders. That sense of accountability is what I want to convey and focus on here. Without that drive and commitment to greater development, we risk HR remaining a service-oriented function rather than a deep-solution-oriented one.

Activating curiosity and sustaining it in oneself and others requires a circular and holistic approach to a growth mindset. As part of our leadership responsibility, we need to think about how to activate curiosity within our teams or in the individuals we partner with.

In addition to using coaching as a way of thinking and problem-solving, we must pay attention to our roles as leaders in culture stewardship. We have the leadership accountability to activate curiosity as leaders by building a curious learning culture.

What does a curious learning culture within an organisation look like? In a curious learning culture, managers or leaders provide their employees with the opportunity to experiment and fail without fear of a negative performance review or judgement. A curious learning culture is, therefore, built on the psychological feeling that it is safe to fail and learn. A curious learning culture is modelled by leaders who demonstrate transparency and open communication, in particular around uncomfortable topics, build trust with their teams, and encourage feedback from a place of improvement and moving forward together as a team.

Real time reflection supports the growth of a curious learning culture. This may look like asking the teams to reflect immediately after a challenging situation or meeting, and consider the refection in real time to capture learnings.

A curious learning culture is full of reflection and inquisitive questions—not assumed correct answers. As leaders, we have the social responsibility to guide and support our teams in achieving their full potential. I believe that activating a sense of curiosity in others and cultivating an environment of openness kick-starts the journey.

When I first moved to Indonesia to take on a new CHRO challenge with a series-B healthcare startup, I knew I had a steep learning curve ahead of me. I had been working in developed countries all my life and knew that moving to an emerging market like Indonesia would present a whole different set of perspectives and challenges—but that is exactly what I wanted.

One thing that I learnt quickly once I immersed myself in my new role in the hustle and bustle of Jakarta was the deep-rooted expectation that leaders have all the answers and that the role of each team is to follow and execute those answers. I often ask:

"What do you think?"

"What is your recommendation?"

"What could the solution look like?"

"What could the impact be?"

"What should we be mindful of?"

The initial shock—which was most often followed by thoughtful and positive reactions—I often receive when I ask the questions above continues to remind me that there are multiple reasons why asking questions in place of providing a solution is powerful. It brings the authenticity of vulnerability, and it activates curiosity in others by allowing a space for exploring answers. Asking questions like the one posed to the payroll manager sends a few different messages of encouragement:

1. I respect your expertise. I think you know the answer or have the ability to find the answer.
2. I, as a leader, do not know everything.
3. I am not going to give you answers when I do not think I have the right approach.

Questions that build on your team's strength and experience builds a learning culture. Learning is a thought process where the past experience and the current learning meet.

Thoughtful questions are powerful ways to trigger individuals to think about their own ability to find solutions to problems, thus activating the loop of curiosity. Thoughtful questions build a curious learning culture with intention.

The practical step to building a curious learning culture with intention is to ask thoughtful reflective inquiry questions.

I learnt from this encounter that the power of questioning transcends geography and culture. It is okay for us to say to our teams that we do not know or understand everything. What matters is that we approach our teams with respect by acknowledging the information they have while showing them that we want to work with them. This is authenticity. If we are being agile in our thinking, then we also want to solicit feedback from our teams when we encounter a problem. Often, they understand the culture and context that we are working within better than anyone. Their thoughts and opinions can help us with our own thinking.

STRATEGY 5: BECOME A GRIT ADVOCATE AND COACH FOR YOUR TEAM

The power of transformation comes from collective action. One of our key roles as people leaders is not only to model a growth mindset for our teams but to actively activate and develop this capacity within our teams.

A practical way to become a grit advocate as a 360-degree leader is to develop your team's grit by making grit tangible. This may look like asking your team to connect with their passion and asking them to list the tangible action items that will develop those passions and identify what a long-term success North Star looks like for your team. You cannot advocate and coach your team without knowing what is meaningful for them. Remember, what is meaningful for you may not carry the same weight for your teams.

Being a grit advocate for your team means that you create a safe space for failure and learning. It means that, even when your team does not deliver, you help them to see the possibilities if they keep trying. Knowing your success North Star helps you to frame your coaching and advocacy for your team. A practical tactic that I have been successfully experimenting with is to normalise failure by overtly calling mistakes and failures "learning/coaching moments" and "missed opportunities." Reframing language is a key to helping your team develop grit and create a safe space for learning.

Once, one of my team members reacted rashly at a request from an employee without clarifying facts. It resulted in confusion and mismanaged expectations around an annual salary increase—and a very upset employee and manager. It was critical to turn the mistake into a coaching moment. The coaching moment looked like this:

1. I listened to the problem and the team's proposed solution.
2. I enquired about the data insights that backed up the solution.
3. I walked the team through the data, which showed the information that was contrary to the information shared.
4. I asked the team member to reassess their recommended solution.
5. I asked the team member for the next steps.
6. I asked the team member for learnings and reflection.

The words "You were wrong" were never uttered.

Being a grit coach for your team also means that you do not have the answers for your team even when you notice that they are steered off course, but you have the questions to redirect them towards finding the appropriate answers. You ask the right questions to help the team grow and develop. It means you take the opportunity to practise the strategies outlined in this book, clear the fog around the concept of a "growth mindset," and capture the tangible opportunity for growth for yourself and the team.

Most importantly, being a grit advocate and coach starts with you role modelling the behaviour. This looks like exercising self-discipline to know where our roadblocks to success are, to eliminate distractions, and to hold routines and habits that will pivot you forward.

REFLECTIVE INQUIRY PRACTICES

- *What are your team members' passions?*
  - *How does it impact their approach to work?*

- *What are your team's roadblocks to success?*
  - *What active role do you play at the moment to support, coach, and advocate your team through the roadblocks*

- *How often do you have overt conversations with your teams on success and failure?*
  - *How do you create an intentional space for your team to share their learnings?*

- *If we were to survey your team, how gritty do you think they think you are?*
  - *How does hypothetical scoring resonate with your own assessment?*

CHAPTER 8

Wrapping It All Up with GROWTH Mindset in Daily Practice

The last two chapters introduced you to the HR growth mindset framework that simplifies and articulates the two fundamental roles of a growth-minded HR: deep-solution architecture and 360-degree leadership, powered by the single most critical capability—a growth mindset, which is cultivated by activating curiosity and practising grit. This framework can be useful when we are thinking and building the capabilities for ourselves and the next generation of HR leaders, and to anchor the longer-term HR transformation, either as a team or as a profession.

On the other hand, such transformation cannot be meaningful without daily practices. The below guide is an articulation of how we can practise a growth mindset daily. When our busy schedules have us juggling multiple issues, we can often find ourselves in a space of reaction rather than growth.

The **GROWTH** model is based on the growth mindset, and it focuses on the thought process of problem-solving. The acronym stands for:

- Go to the space of curiosity
- Reconnect with the problem space
- Omit the best practice mindset
- Win together
- T-shaped learning
- Harvest grit and curiosity

The GROWTH model provides a relatively simple framework for the problem-solving process by channelling a growth mindset, independent of the context of the HR profession.

The GROWTH model seeks to serve as a reminder that we, as HR professionals, can make a sustainable change that evolves us and those around us. The GROWTH-minded HR takes an active and reflective approach to problem-solving and leadership. GROWTH-minded HR is the capability to activate grit and curiosity as part of your career journey and daily practice.

✳ ✳ ✳

GO TO THE SPACE OF CURIOSITY

This serves as the reminder that when we are presented with problems, the activation of our curiosity requires us to continue seeking the space for that curiosity to happen. It may look like asking more questions, it may look like doing more research, but it definitely does not look like jumping into the first instinct to answer straight away.

RECONNECT WITH THE PROBLEM SPACE

Understand that most problems at the surface level do not capture the depth and complexity of the problem. Asking more questions to truly dive into the root of the problem provides the foundation for the solution that is the most impactful and sustainable.

OMIT THE BEST PRACTICE MINDSET

Most of the problems we tackle have best practices or previous solutions available from somewhere. Viewing best practices not as an actual solution outcome but as a fixed mindset that seeks the comfort of the best approved and appreciated solution requires you to sit with the discomfort of not knowing and experimenting with different potential solutions and outcomes.

WIN TOGETHER

The most interesting and complex problems are never solved alone. Actively seeking out others to collaborate and problem-solve together is an active approach to practise curiosity and humility. We do not have all the answers. Think about who else can be the appropriate partner to work with you on the problem and provide insights that differ from yours. This is a great time to actively and intentionally seek input from those that have very different experiences or views from you.

T-SHAPED LEARNING

When we have deep expertise and experiences, we are often trapped in viewing problem-solving through the lens we know best. The deeper we are connected to an expertise, the higher the likelihood that we face problems through a single dimension. T-shaped learning recognises the need to learn more broadly because it allows us to consider problems in a multi-dimensional way. This may look like asking ourselves, "What could the opposite view look like? What would other experts in different areas of expertise say from their own expert lens?"

HARVEST GRIT AND CURIOSITY

In the world of complex problem-solving, we not only do not have all the answers, but our attempts and experiments to solve problems may also lack the traction and impact we envisioned. How we continue to learn from the experiment and keep tackling the problem becomes our grit and curiosity practice that cultivates a growth mindset. This may look like taking a step back and learning from our failures. It requires us not to take failure personally and not lose sight of the outcomes intended by solving the problem.

* * *

Channelling a growth mindset feels uncomfortable.

It should feel uncomfortable as GROWTH takes us on a path to the future and not a static state as we solve complex and meaningful problems on behalf of our employees, team, leaders, organisations, and community.

By recognising the power of being a growth-minded HR, we are able to reimagine HR through the lens of a growth mindset, where we take on the fundamental role of a deep-solution architect and a well-rounded 360-degree leader. By taking a growth approach to our profession, we feel empowered to explore outside the comfort of best practices and find a deeper connection with our own growth as HR leaders while providing new insights through our HR practices. We are no longer an executional function but the driving force behind growth mindset activation for those around us. We become advocates of our craft and professions, and feel a sense of pride in the impact we are able to realise with growth practices.

By using the GROWTH model for problem-solving, we ask questions we have never asked before and provide solutions above and beyond the comfort zone of best practices. We continue to introduce and refine growth practices and build suitable solutions for the problems we are solving together. The GROWTH model also reminds us that learning is circular, and we must continue to harvest grit and curiosity through our learning and share those learnings.

We must become role models for our team and leaders to cultivate a growth mindset and embrace the collective power of reimagination.

Conclusion

If anything, this book is a testament to the power of the growth mindset when it is full of curiosity and grit. It took more than three years to write. That journey took two relocations, three jobs, two degrees, and one baby to complete. To a large extent, I have always felt that the journey of book ideation, researching, and writing is itself so full of learning that publication is only the cherry on top.

However, as I continue to learn and evolve in my own HR career and personal transformation with a focus on developing and mentoring the next generation of HR, I realise that completing and publishing this book is another form of my own growth mindset practice because it allows me to articulate and share what I have learnt and to learn by sharing. The challenge in knowledge sharing is finding a balance between evoking and activating reflective thought processes and enabling the reader to learn in their own space and extrapolation. Plus, there is getting over the sense of arrogance that comes with telling a story from a first-person perspective! By no means does this book have all the answers to drive future HR transformation, nor does it present ideas with the same academic rigour as peer-reviewed articles.

This book presents a reflective view of HR as a profession and attempts to clarify concepts pertaining to operating models and operating principles/approaches. I have aimed to provide some clarity by looking back at the evolution of HR as a field and defining—or redefining—some of its key concepts. I take a macro approach first and then dive deeper into individual growth mindset strategies. To a large extent, the second part of this book advocates for a personal and practical approach to cultivating a growth mindset in the context of HR, regardless of the operating model. I present a clear vision for the future of HR, independent of the operating model that one may find themselves working within.

Furthermore, I articulate the fundamental belief that we should build on what we can influence. We do not always find ourselves in the position to influence and change organisational or functional operating principles and models. What we have influence over is how we manage our own careers and mindsets.

As we come to the end of this book, I sit here with excitement for what the future brings for HR and the evolving workforce that we continue to advocate for.

I hope this book provides some actionable strategies and thought-provoking ideas for you. As a call to action, I would love to continue to learn from your reflective inquiry practices. Please reach out and share with me as we continue to revise the book and we learn and grow as a profession together.

With that, I sign off with a quote from the researcher that pioneers the concept of growth mindset, Carol Dweck:

"Real self-confidence is not reflected in a title, an expensive suit, a fancy car, or a series of acquisitions. It is reflected in your mindset: your readiness to grow."

I sincerely hope your growth mindset will enable your curiosity to dive deep into the problem that you are trying to solve, with your grit as the cornerstone to your sustained thinking and deep learning.

Happy growing!

About the Author

For nearly two decades, Susan has worked with teams and leaders to develop talent strategies and interventions that build capabilities for sustainable growth across a broad range of companies. Susan believes in the power of human resources as a function to transform business outcomes and people experiences.

Susan has worked with diverse companies, including a healthcare startup in Indonesia, the first decacorn technology platform in Indonesia that went public, a fintech multinational company in Singapore, a national energy company in Norway, and a gaming and entertainment company headquartered in the United States.

Susan is also a strong advocate for education transformation and inclusion, and has worked and lived in Taiwan, New Zealand, the United Kingdom, Norway, Singapore, and Indonesia. Susan holds the people investment thesis that the fundamental growth of human potential can only be unlocked and amplified through a growth mindset. Susan is also a strategic advisor and angel investor in various education and people technology startups searching to transform learner impact and learning and career outcomes.

Susan received her PhD with a focus on knowledge management from the University of Stavanger, Norway, and is continuing further capability development in the areas of educational psychology, education technology, and research.

Appendix

Reflective inquiry practices in consolidation.

PART I

CHAPTER 1

Some useful dimensions to think through as you are articulating your organisational HR philosophy include:

- *What are our organisational values?*
- *What are the behaviours that we do not want to endorse?*
- *What do our companies' compensation and benefits say about us?*
- *Are our HR policies and processes aligned with our organisational HR philosophy?*

Some useful questions to ask yourself:

- *How do I see the role of HR?*
- *What type of HR leader do I aspire to be?*

- *What part of my current environment do I struggle with when practising HR?*
- *What are my non-negotiables when I am designing HR solution recommendations?*

PART II
CHAPTER 3

Some reflective inquiry practices questions that could be useful to identify your growth mindset blind spots are:

- *What was my last attempt to learn something that failed? What have I learnt from that?*
- *What was my last attempt to learn something that succeeded? What have I learnt from that?*
- *How do I feel when I receive negative feedback about my work?*
- *What do I do when I receive negative feedback about my work?*
- *How do I keep going when I am stuck on a problem?*
- *In what environment do I learn the best?*

Reflective Inquiry Practices

- *What is your growth mindset blind spot?*
- *How has the blind spot shown up in your life and career as an HR leader?*

CHAPTER 5
Reflective Inquiry Practices

- *What are you learning at the moment? Or what would you like to be learning?*

- *What was the last learning medium that you enjoyed (or currently enjoy)?*
- *What does your learning habit look like at present?*
- *How much time can you reasonably commit to learning a week?*

Reflective Inquiry Practices

- *Pay attention the next time someone comes to you with a problem. What mindset do you gravitate towards?*
  - *What is usually your first sentence after someone has shared a problem with you?*
- *Reflect on how well you actively listen by making a conscious review of these six components: pay attention, withhold judgement, reflect, clarify, summarise, and share.*
  - *What are the conditions that allow you to be deeper in your active listening?*

Reflective Inquiry Practices

- *How do you feel when someone speaks about best practice solutions?*
- *What does "experimenting" look like and mean for you? What does "experimenting" look like and mean for your teams and/ or organisation?*
  - *Is there a gap in perception?*
- *On a scale of one to ten (ten being the highest), how much do you enjoy experiments?*

CHAPTER 6
Reflective Inquiry Practices

Find out how gritty you are using the Grit Scale, developed by Angela Duckworth:

	NOT AT ALL	NOT MUCH	SOMEWHAT	MOSTLY	VERY MUCH
New ideas and projects sometimes distract me from previous ones.	5	4	3	2	1
Setbacks don't discourage me. I don't give up easily.	1	2	3	4	5
I often set a goal but later choose to pursue a different one.	5	4	3	2	1
I am a hard worker.	1	2	3	4	5
I have difficulty maintaining my focus on projects that take more than a few months to complete.	5	4	3	2	1
I finish whatever I begin.	1	2	3	4	5
My interests change from year to year.	5	4	3	2	1
I am diligent. I never give up.	1	2	3	4	5
I have been obsessed with a certain idea or project for a short time but later lost interest.	5	4	3	2	1
I have overcome setbacks to conquer an important challenge.	1	2	3	4	5

Add up all the points for the boxes you checked and divide by ten to receive your Grit Score. The maximum score you can achieve is five (extremely gritty), and the lowest score is one (not at all gritty). Use the chart below to see how your score compares to others. (For example, a score of 2.5 reveals that you are grittier than just 10 per cent of the population.)

PERCENTILE	GRIT SCORE
10%	2.5
20%	3.0
30%	3.3
40%	3.5
50%	3.8
60%	3.9
70%	4.1
80%	4.3
90%	4.5
95%	4.7
99%	4.9

- *What are you passionate about?*
  - *When was the last time you failed when you did something you are passionate about?*
  - *What did you learn from your failure?*
- *What does your passion mean to you?*
  - *What does your passion mean for others close to you?*
- *How would you describe your passion and its impact in one sentence?*
- *What are your areas of interest?*
  - *Can you articulate how your interests differ from your passion?*

- *Explore and discover. What is your most productive time?*
  - *How much of that time would you devote to learning every week?*
- *Start a learning journal.*
  - *What do you keep track of?*

- *What did your upbringing teach you about success?*
  - *How have you carried that through your life?*
- *How does failure make you feel?*
  - *When was the last time you shared your failures openly?*
  - *How did that may you feel?*
- *How does criticism make you feel?*
- *What is your first instinct when someone says, "May I share feedback with you?"*

- *Articulate what "everyday grittiness" looks like to you.*
- *Find three people who fit that description.*
- *Craft out time to be with those you consider gritty*

PART III
CHAPTER 7
Reflective Inquiry Practices

- *What are three of your go-to reflective questions? Create them and try them out!*
- *How does it feel? Does it feel different than before? How?*

Reflective Inquiry Practices

- *On a scale of one to ten (ten being the highest), how comfortable are you with not having all the right answers at your immediate disposal?*
- *Practise the one question and one probing statement technique.*
  - *How did it go?*
  - *What are some probing statements that are powerful for you?*

Reflective Inquiry Practices

- *On a scale of one to ten (ten being the highest), how would you describe the power dynamics between the business and the HR department where you work?*
- *How does the language you use day to day contribute to that?*
  - *What is one word/term that you would like to see change in your current context?*

- *What is the role of HR in your organisational learning?*
- *What does learning mean to you?*
- *How can we activate learning in ways that are not programmatic in nature?*

- *Articulate your authentic self as a leader.*
  - *When are you at your best?*
  - *When are you at your worst?*

- *What is the one core principle/value that you stand by in life?*
- *How do you usually react when someone criticises your work? Does this align with how you think you should react?*
- *When was the last time you asked, "What do you think?" to your team or to others with opposing views? What was that experience like?*
- *Invite someone who is close to you professionally to share their observations of you. Compare these to our own image of yourself. Are there any gaps?*

References

PART I: HR TRANSFORMATION—A TRANSFORMATION THAT NEVER ENDS
CHAPTER 1: A GLIMPSE INTO THE HISTORICAL EVOLUTION OF HR—PAST, PRESENT, AND FUTURE

Canales, Katie. "Tony Hsieh, the Late Former CEO of Zappos, Famously Pioneered the Concept of Paying New, Unhappy Employees $2,000 to Quit in Order to Maintain a Happy, Productive Workforce." Insider, November 30, 2020. https://www.businessinsider.com/zappos-tony-hsieh-paid-new-workers-to-quit-the-offer-2020-11.

Cunningham, Lillian, "Accenture CEO Explains Why He's Overhauling Performance Reviews." *The Washington Post*, July 23, 2015. https://www.washingtonpost.com/news/on-leadership/wp/2015/07/23/accenture-ceo-explains-the-reasons-why-hes-overhauling-performance-reviews/.

Davis, Nicholas. "What Is the Fourth Industrial Revolution?" World Economic Forum. January 19, 2016. https://www.weforum.org/agenda/2016/01/what-is-the-fourth-industrial-revolution/.

Dean, Grace. "Google Is Scrapping Its Famous, Lavish Staff Buffets as Its Reopens its Offices, but Employees Can Still Get Free Food." Insider, April 30, 2021. https://www.businessinsider.com/google-free-food-staff-scraps-buffet-us-offices-catering-alphabet-2021-4.

Dictionary.com, s.v. "best practice (n.)." Accessed November 4, 2022. https://www.dictionary.com/browse/best-practice.

Grossmeier, Jessica, Ray Fabius, Jennifer P. Flynn, Steven P. Noeldner, Dan Fabius, Ron Z. Goetzel, and David R. Anderson. "Linking Workplace Health Promotion Best Practices and Organizational Financial Performance: Tracking Market Performance of Companies with Highest Scores on the HERO Scorecard." Journal of Occupational and Environmental Medicine 58, no. 1 (January 2016): 16–23. https://doi.org/10.1097/jom.0000000000000631.

McCord, Patty. "How Netflix Reinvented HR." Harvard Business Review, January–February 2014. https://hbr.org/2014/01/how-netflix-reinvented-hr.

Schwab, Klaus. Fourth Industrial Revolution. Geneva: World Economic Forum, 2016.

Singapore Human Resources Institute home page. Accessed November 4, 2022. https://shri.org.sg/.

Society for Human Resources Management home page. Accessed November 4, 2022. https://www.shrm.org/.

Ulrich, David. "HR's Reinvention: Moving from Benchmarking and Best Practices to Guidance." LinkedIn, January 12, 2021. https://www.linkedin.com/pulse/hrs-reinvention-moving-from-benchmarking-best-practices-dave-ulrich/.

PART II: CURIOSITY AND GRIT: LEVERS TO CULTIVATE A GROWTH MINDSET

CHAPTER 3: FOSTER SELF-REFLECTION HABITS AS THE STARTING POINT FOR A GROWTH MINDSET

Dweck, Carol S. *Mindset: The New* Psychology *of Success*. New York: Random House, 2006.

Dweck, Carol. "What Having a 'Growth Mindset' Actually Means." *Harvard Business Review*, January 13, 2016. https://hbr.org/2016/01/ what-having-a-growth-mindset-actually-means.

Larson, Carylynn. "The Challenges of Adopting a Coaching Mindset, and How Leaders Can Overcome Them." Forbes Coaches Council, *Forbes*, April 24, 2019. https://www. forbes.com/sites/forbescoachescouncil/2019/04/24/ the-challenges-of-adopting-a-coaching-mindset-and-how-leaders-can-overcome-them/?sh=c02fb2610acc.

Leading Effectively Staff, "How to Use Active Listening Skills to Coach Others." Center for Creative Leadership. December 2, 2021. https://www.ccl.org/articles/leading-effectively-articles/ coaching-others-use-active-listening-skills/.

CHAPTER 4: A GROWTH MINDSET IS CULTIVATED BY TWO CORNERSTONE CAPABILITIES—CURIOSITY AND GRIT

Cambridge Dictionary, s.v. "curiosity (*n.*)." Accessed November 4, 2022. https://dictionary.cambridge.org/us/dictionary/english/curiosity.

Chen, Susan P. "Forget Teaching Hard and Soft Skills. Activate Employee Curiosity Instead!" LinkedIn, August 11, 2019. https://www.linkedin.com/pulse/ forget-skills-teach-employees-curiosity-instead-susan-p-chen-ph-d-/.

Geiger, Christy. "Curiosity: Why It Matters, Why We Lose It, and How to Get It Back." Forbes Coaches Council, *Forbes*, June 1, 2021. https://www.forbes.com/sites/forbescoachescouncil/2021/06/01/curiosity-why-it-matters-why-we-lose-it-and-how-to-get-it-back/?sh=6aa77da22fa4.

George, Steve. "Competence and Competency Frameworks Fact Sheet." Chartered Institute of Personnel and Development. Last updated December 15, 2021. https://www.cipd.co.uk/knowledge/fundamentals/people/performance/competency-factsheet.

Grant, Adam. *Originals: How Non-Conformists Move the World*. New York: Viking Penguin, 2016.

Linker, Maureen. *Intellectual Empathy: Critical Thinking for Social Justice*. Ann Arbor: University of Michigan Press, 2015.

CHAPTER 5: STRATEGIES TO ACTIVATE CURIOSITY

Ng, Sik Hung, and Fei Deng, "Language and Power." In *Oxford Research Encyclopedia of Communication*. August 22, 2017. https://doi.org/10.1093/acrefore/9780190228613.013.436.

CHAPTER 6: STRATEGIES TO PRACTISE GRIT

"Grit Scale." Angela Duckworth. Accessed November 4, 2022. https://angeladuckworth.com/grit-scale/.

Clear, James. Atomic Habits: An Easy & Proven Way to Build Good Habits & Break Bad Ones. New York: Avery, 2018.

Duckworth, Angela. *Grit: The Power of Passion and Perseverance*. New York: Scribner, 2019.

Frey, Aline, and Marie-Line Bosse. "Perceptual Span, Visual Span, and Visual Attention Span: Three Potential Ways to Quantify Limits on Visual Processing During Reading." *Visual Cognition* 26, no. 6 (2018): 412–429. https://doi.org/10.1080/13506285.2018.1472163.

Hennessey, Corissa. "The Growth Mindset: How Intelligence Can Change and Grow." Connections Academy. April 5, 2022. https://www.connectionsacademy.com/support/resources/article/the-growth-mind-set-how-intelligence-can-change-and-grow/. [The questions in this chapter were adapted from Yes, Inc.'s "Questions to Encourage Growth Mindset."]

Neal, David T., Wendy Wood, and Jeffrey M. Quinn. "Habits—A Repeat Performance." *Current Directions in Psychological Science* 15, no. 4 (August 2006): 931–959. https://doi.org/10.1111/j.1467-8721.2006.00435.x.

Schmidhuber, Jürgen. "Deep Learning in Neural Networks: An Overview." *Neural Networks* 61 (January 2015): 85–117. https://doi.org/10.1016/j.neunet.2014.09.003.

PART III: BRINGING IT ALL TOGETHER
CHAPTER 7: INTRODUCING THE HR GROWTH MINDSET FRAMEWORK

Meginley, Dave. "9 Competencies for HR Excellence." *HR Certification Institute* (blog). February 14, 2022. https://www.hrci.org/community/blogs-and-announcements/hr-leads-business-blog/hr-leads-business/2020/09/04/nine-competencies-for-hr-excellence-emerge.

CHAPTER 8: WRAPPING IT ALL UP WITH GROWTH MINDSET IN DAILY PRACTICE

Epstein, David. Range: Why Generalists Triumph in a Specialized World. New York: Riverhead Books, 2019.